CO-ATM-627

Social Theory and Social Practice

Social Theory and Social Practice

HANS L. ZETTERBERG

The Bedminster Press   New York   1 9 6 2

Copyright © 1962
The Bedminster Press
New York
Library of Congress Catalog Card Number: 61–18319

Manufactured in the United States of America
by H. Wolff, New York

HV
31
.Z4

Contents

Alma College Library
Alma, Michigan

Preface

This book wants to set forth a program, not accomplishments. It deals with accomplishments of practical sociology only to the extent that they illustrate the need of the program (Chapter 2) and the feasibility of the program (Chapter 4). The achievements of theoretical sociology are sketched in somewhat fuller detail (Chapter 3) but a documentation of these accomplishments must await a general treatise on theoretical sociology; the present statement is merely a prospectus.

It is easy to say "tulip," but hard to make one. In sociology, programmatic ideas are common and workable ideas are rare. The program advocated here suggests that applied sociology should proceed from the client's problem to something very abstract—theoretical problems and theoretical solutions—and then back to the client's problem with a practical solution. Thus it disagrees with two widely held conceptions: that applied social science consists of applied research projects, and that social science is put to work by a popularization of its content. Instead, the program advocated here is one of applied social theory.

It is still debatable to what extent this is a workable program. It was first put forth in a memorandum in 1956–57. A respected American colleague said then that "its ideas, even if right in principle, do not suit the pragmatic approach of American social scientists." A respected European colleague considered its methodology of translating theory into practical advice "much less important than the methodology of theory construction and the methodology of research," and he used his editorial prerogatives to cut down the memorandum to a third its size when it was submitted as part of a general essay on theory, method and practice in sociology. The Ford Foundation, which had given a small grant to have these ideas developed, with the prospect of nursing them along with new grants, did not support the matter further. The Bureau of Applied Social Research at Columbia University, where they had been written, did not want to house consultations based on these premises. Reluctantly I agreed to consider the whole enterprise as one of the many false starts that are part of academic life and scholarship.

However, in the five years since this program of applied theory was formalized, I have had the opportunity to do a few sociological consultations on practical problems. While some consultations have been more successful than others, I have become more convinced that the program is workable. The proof of this must await the compilation of a number of cases in which it has been used. But I am now confident enough about it to present a revised version of the approach itself to a larger public.

Professor Robert K. Merton helped me to take the first steps in analyzing the process by means of which academic knowledge can be used by practitioners, and Professors Charles Y. Glock and James S. Coleman also participated in the early discussions that formulated the objectives of bringing theory and practice together by reorganizing academic knowledge for practical use. These discussions were full of imagination and inspiration and indispensable to this enterprise. I also want to thank Charles Emery and Roger Walcott, who in 1956 were research assistants in the Bureau of Applied Social Research, working on this project. Mr. Emery interviewed thirty practitioners about one hundred problems and Mr. Walcott abstracted a large number of books written for practitioners, and both helped in the analysis of what goes on when knowledge guides practice. Finally, I want to thank Dr. Jan van der Marck, who served as a special consultant on matters of art, and Mrs. Ingrid E. Galtung, who in 1958 was my co-worker on the art museum study which I have drawn upon at length as an illustration of the approach this book wants to promote.

HANS L. ZETTERBERG

Columbia University
New York

Social Theory and Social Practice

1 The Problem

One of the most appealing ideas of our century is the notion that science can be put to work to provide solutions to social problems. If eighteenth-century physics gave us the modern engineer to deal with technological problems, and nineteenth-century biology gave us the modern physician to deal with health problems, so twentieth-century social science dreams that it shall give mankind the social practitioner to deal scientifically with social problems.

Encouragement of this dream comes primarily from the increasing volume of social research and from the increasing ranks of practitioners of social science. Yet it is a frustrating dream. The professional literature contains hundreds of sociological research papers in which the conclusion calls for further research, but only a handful in which the conclusion calls for practical actions. The numbers of social practitioners listed in the census—social, group, recreation, and welfare workers and persons employed in personnel and labor relations —have increased at a faster rate than the rest of the labor force, but the actual practice in welfare and personnel does not seem to have changed appreciably.[1]

More important, the gap between theoretical knowledge and practical action remains wide. When a client approaches an academic scientist with the phrase "I have a problem . . ." he usually gets the answer, "Let's do research about it . . ." A large number of social research organizations have appeared during the past two decades in which this type of exchange is quite frequent. It attests to the fact that social research has come of age and is able to give guidance to those who deal with social problems of various sorts. We are usually so delighted over this fact that it rarely occurs to us that this type of exchange also attests to a fundamental immaturity of social science.

1 In both theoretical and practical sociology, we tend to substitute actual progress by changing our technical vocabulary every decade. A social theorist of 1930 would hardly understand a social theorist talking in the vocabulary of 1960, and a social worker of 1930 would hardly understand a description of social practice in the professional language of 1960. Yet the theorist's actual knowledge and the practitioner's actual action are likely to be very much the same at both times.

16

However, when a patient approaches a physician or an industrialist approaches an engineer with the phrase "I have a problem," the response, "Let's do research about it," is not at all common. The physician and the engineer can, in most instances, rely on already codified knowledge to give help and advice. It is indeed ludicrous to think of a situation in which a contemporary engineer proposes to do research to discover the laws of mechanics when he is consulted about the building of a bridge, or a situation in which a contemporary physician embarks on a research program to discover insulin when consulted about diabetes. But the social scientist is happy to suggest a project about the causes of prejudice when consulted about an interracial housing project. The fact that the social scientist says, "Let's do research about it," signals his common inability to draw upon codified knowledge when faced with a new practical problem. We have competent researchers but hardly any competent consultants.

Now, of course, social problems cry for solutions and cannot normally wait for science to develop the appropriate laws or furnish the relevant information. Even when research funds are available, the scientific proofs demand long investments of time, and the time is often scarce when the cry "Do something!" is in the air. Thus, practitioners and consultants are frequently called into action to give scientific solutions when such solutions hardly exist. In their prescriptions for and treatment of a social problem, these practitioners and consultants, therefore, have to mix whatever confirmed generalizations they remember from past teaching or reading with their personal and professional traditions, prejudices, and insights. This is not necessarily an undesirable state of affairs; all societies must, of course, deal with their exigencies and emergencies, and this is perhaps the best we can do at present. Nor is it unique to the social practitioner; medicine and engineering still encounter similar dilemmas.

Yet it is most legitimate to ask the question: What can be done to insure that the established knowledge we have is actually used in social practice?

What is missing is not helpful practitioners. We have numerous men and women of good will with a real knack for solving social problems. What is missing is rather "competent" practitioners, competent in translating scientific theory into practice. The defining characteristic of a scientifically competent practitioner is not his contribution to scientific knowledge and methodology, but his use of scientific knowledge in solving problems repeatedly encountered in his occupation.

It may be worth noting that in other sciences *handbooks for practitioners* have appeared which facilitate the use of available knowledge. They differ from theoretical treatises summarizing the same knowledge in that they are organized, not to achieve maximum parsimony of propositions, but to achieve maximum finger-tip knowledge for a practitioner who is faced with a specific problem. In medicine, textbooks of anatomy and physiology have existed for hundreds of years. However, it was not until 1892, when the first edition of Sir William Osler's *Principles and Practice of Medicine* appeared, that an effective way of presenting this knowledge for the use of the practicing physician was found. It has been claimed that this book reshaped medical practice, and that more medical students have learned diagnosis and treatment from it than from any other text. Yet, it is only fair to say that the impact of this book is not due primarily to its ideas: rather, it is due to the organization of its ideas. Thus, the format of this book will serve well to illustrate how knowledge has been successfully codified for use in medical practice.[2]

The book is centered around a series of classifications of diseases. Each section deals with a class of anatomically and/or physiologically interrelated diseases, for example, "diseases of the digestive system," "diseases of the respiratory system." The material pertinent to each disease in a section is then presented in a standardized fashion. In broad outline, this standardized arrangement consists of a selection from the following categories:

[2] This was suggested to me by Professor Robert K. Merton.

Definition of the disease: here we are usually given a short compact statement describing the disease.

History of knowledge and treatment: a brief résumé about scientific progress and past errors experienced by medical science in dealing with the disease.

Incidence: under this heading we find major epidemiological data about the disease.

Etiology: here we learn about predispositions and causes of the disease. Sometimes this section is followed by one on bacteriology, infection and immunity.

Symptoms: this is a section presenting the typical course of the illness, its special features and its particular physical signs as objectively manifested, or reported by the patient. Easily recognized anatomical difficulties and lesions which are associated with the disease are presented and described.

Prognosis: under this heading identifiable variations and complications are discussed and consequences for different kinds of patients are pointed out. Sometimes this is followed by a section on relapses or on associations with other diseases.

Diagnosis: in this category explicit directions are given as to *where* the physician should look, *what* he should look for in order to identify a disease and what kind of tests he can use to aid in the diagnosis.

Treatment: here instructions are given about what to do about the disease. Occasionally a word is said also about prophylaxis.

20

The medical knowledge presented in this book is *not* primarily organized around the theoretical propositions of anatomy, histology, physiology, etc. Rather it is centered around the needs of the situation in which a physician examines a patient. In a standardized fashion Osler tells the physician *where* he shall look, *what* he shall look for, and, dependent on what he finds, *how* he shall treat the patient. At the same time the author reminds the physician of the relevant knowledge acquired in the systematic study of anatomy, histology, physiology, etc., and he may even give a reference to the history of this knowledge.

It is a matter of historical record that Osler's categories in an excellent way link medical knowledge to the real life situation of the physician faced with a patient in trouble. The value of this format is demonstrated particularly by its persistence through repeated editions into which the new medical knowledge of the last half-century has been fitted. It might be noted that not all of the above categories are used in the description of every disease, partly because of lack of knowledge, a fact which Osler often attests. In this way the format also reveals where more research and better theory are needed and suggests one form of interplay between research, theory and practice.

I do not believe we can have anything as standardized as this format in social science, since most social practitioners do not meet their clients under such standard-ized conditions as do the physicians. But it should be possible for us social practitioners in the 1960s to use as much of the available sociological knowledge in our practice as Osler's students used available medical knowledge in the 1890s. We, too, must find ways to for-mulate what we know so that it becomes relevant to the problems with which we deal. I believe the following is true:

1. There is a body of seasoned sociological knowl-edge, summarized as principles of theoretical sociology, which is superior to our common-sense notions about society.

2. Social practitioners are not consciously and sys-tematically using this body of knowledge in their pro-fessional activities.

3. There is, however, a general formula or schema that can be used to make theoretical knowledge help practitioners in solving social problems.

The chapters that follow are devoted to these three theses.

2 The Knowledge of Social Practitioners

To what extent do social practitioners use scientific knowledge on their jobs? This delicate question can best be answered by observing them in practice. Lacking this possibility, we might consider the quality of their professional training. Schools for practitioners give as a matter of course more or less extensive training in basic social science. Much specific knowledge from the school years might be only vaguely remembered in later practice, but here as elsewhere, the rule holds that education is what is left when we have forgotten everything we learned. That is, long after the specific pieces of knowledge are forgotten, certain generalizations and habits of thought remain. For example, the social worker in an adoption agency may forget much about the detailed information concerning heredity and might not be able to recall a single scientific study of the topic, but the generalization that "acquired characteristics are not hereditary" will remain with her and be of considerable use in her professional practice. No judgment about the knowledge of professionals should overlook such latent effects of past scientific instruction.

A more general idea of the extent to which practitioners rely upon scientific knowledge can be obtained by an examination of the literature they read. We interviewed thirty practitioners and corresponded with an additional thirty asking them to name the articles or books that had been most helpful to them as practitioners. We emphasized that we wanted to know about useful books, preferably how-to-do-it books. The titles mentioned by the respondents are listed at the end of this chapter. The list presumably represents the scientific literature of the social practitioners at its best. For one thing, we asked them to mention only the most helpful books; for another, we did not ask a representative sample of practitioners, but rather picked some who seemed likely to be most informed, experienced, and advanced.

We have made a brief examination of the titles in this bibliography to see to what extent they contain practical advice based on recognized scientific knowledge. The result is a complex one. While it is clearly negative for the most part, much of scientific or practical value is nevertheless found in these books. Using as a criterion reliance upon systematic knowledge, we can classify the practitioner literature in five groupings.

Professional Creeds

Books written for practitioners often begin with statements of the moral credo that underlies professional practice. These statements present in general terms the ethical, and occasionally political, objectives of professional practice. Also, in a broad way, they indicate what are the morally approved means to realize these objectives. As an example we can select the following "Basic Assumptions of Group Work" as they are presented in a text for social workers:

A group worker is neither a propagandist nor a manipulator. He interprets and makes available the resources of the agency including its outlook on life as expressed in agency objectives. Because his first concern is always the opportunity for self-directed growth he does not coerce people . . .

The program must be seen always in terms of its effect on individuals. This involves, in the first place, keeping his relation to the group person-centered and not activity-centered. Success from the group worker's point of view is seen

Social Theory and Social Practice

. . . in terms of what the experience means to the participants.[1]

The "theory" of group work set forth here is a norma-
tive theory. It serves to give a social, moral, or political
legitimization of professional practice, not a scientific
legitimization.

However, to the extent that professional creeds evolve
around the means and ends of professional practice, they
also involve matters of empirical knowledge. To say
that we shall use means M to reach our goal G, implies
that we take the proposition "if M, then G" to be true.
The group worker is told to assume that if she persuades
rather than coerces, then self-directed personalities will
emerge in her group. This is plausible enough. However, it is typical that statements of professional creeds
rarely make explicit these assumptions and never cite
scientific studies that support them. To the knowledgeable scientist these creeds, therefore, often appear tenuous or oversimplified. Historians can cite many examples of how self-directed men emerged under conditions
of great coercion, and the social psychologist, familiar
with experiments on leadership climates, will maintain
that persuasion per se is irrelevant. The effect is produced through one kind, e.g., democratic persuasion,

1 Grace Coyle, *Group Work with American Youth* (New York: Harpers,
1948), pp. 25, 27–28.

28

but negligible with another kind, e.g., authoritarian persuasion.

Case Studies

A case study is a descriptive account of a past problem situation. It tells what happened, what the practitioners did, and how the situation changed. Analysis of the principles at work are missing, and no special attempt is made to classify the various facts that comprise the description. Case studies seem important particularly where a large number of components, often interrelated in highly intricate ways, may be very difficult to measure and classify, but they can be quickly grasped on an intuitive basis. When they are presented as compact, rather nontechnical descriptions, the reader is provided with a large store of problem-relevant (although unsystematic) knowledge.

Case histories provide vicarious experience. When faced with problems similar to those reported in the case studies, practitioners might consider the solutions that were reported as effective in the case study. The facts of the case history through a process of induction become generalizations, and these generalizations through a process of deductions are applied to the new case at hand. This, of course, can be very useful. The trouble is that the whole procedure is usually "intuitive"; that is, the inductions are never formulated, no limiting conditions are stated for the generalizations, and no deduction to the new problem is made explicit. Thus, the possibilities of error multiply.

An illustration of the use of case studies can be drawn from a report entitled "Maintenance of Morale and Production in Routine Clerical Work":

The Benefits Payment Section of the Pennsylvania Bureau of Employment and Unemployment Compensation has a Computing Unit that is engaged in determining the financial elegibility of claimants for unemployment compensation.

[The work of the unit was divided into two computing steps, each to be done by a different clerk.] After about two years the employees had acquired the maximum skill in the operation of the computing machines or in the use of the charts. With the attainment of stationary performance, the work began to seem monotonous and tedious.

The change in procedure was worked out which combined the two steps in the computing process so that the same employees could carry through the entire computation. There was no variation in the initial steps of cross-adding, totaling the quarters' earnings, and dividing by eight.

Morale of the staff has become excellent. During rush periods there is friendly rivalry in the unit, all striving to be at the top in production with a minimum of error.[2]

2 *Case Reports in Public Administration* (Social Science Research Council: New York), Vol. 2, No. 57.

Here we have an incident in which a reduction in the division of labor resulted in higher morale and better production speed. The practitioner can read this, and more or less explicitly draw the conclusion: when clerks, each doing a short piece of a total operation, get bored or slow, let them each do a longer piece of the operation. However, the social theorist, familiar with the long tradition of thought about division of labor, would be unable to accept the general validity of such a proposition. In a slightly different situation, Durkheim's theory on this topic would suggest that an increase in the division of labor, making for further mutual dependence, would improve morale and give it a different quality.[3] Furthermore, the scientist would be unable to endorse the idea that there is a direct relationship between morale and productivity. Experiments have demonstrated that morale only increases the power of the group over the members.[4] There is no guarantee that the group will use this power to speed up production. Indeed, increased morale may slow down production if the informal norms of the work group prescribe production restrictions.

In all, the use of case studies by practitioners may be

---

3 Emile Durkheim, *De la division du travail social* (Felix Alcan: Paris, 1893).

4 Stanley Schachter *et al.,* "An Experimental Study of Cohesiveness and Productivity," *Human Relations,* IV (1951), pp. 229–238.

suggestive, but it is a procedure too full of pitfalls to have the reliability we associate with science.

Rules of Thumb

Occasionally someone who has worked actively in a field as a practitioner sets down accumulated experiences for others in the same field. The basis for knowledge here is pragmatic: what practices have been successful? Discussions of "common mistakes" bring out the trial and error quality of this kind of knowledge. These books of rules of thumb do not refer to the principles of academic social science; they are based instead on the experiences of the author and the practices of his or her organization.

Such a book might help a practitioner to introduce an element of orderliness in his job situation and point up considerations that might be overlooked by the unwary practitioner. Most of the books of this kind we looked at, however, were marred by an enthused triviality and fell short of the more exact statements most practical situations would demand. Consider, for example, the subject of committees in a book for administrators in social work and education:

We know that group members must be compatible to a certain degree and that they must feel a part of the group.

Is this not another essential? The composition of our committees is of great significance . . .

We know that groups require leadership skilled in the art of helping people relate to one another and to the tasks at hand. Is chairmanship not one of the keys to the committee? Chairmen must be carefully selected and trained.[5]

Here the author points out some problems, but his solutions are vague. It is impossible from these comments to learn how to recognize "compatible" group members and "skilled" leaders, much less how to pick them. At the point where we really need advice we are left dangling in mid-air.

Better rule-of-thumb statements can also be found. For example, in a personnel officer's training manual for foremen, we find an account of the way in which a foreman is taught to handle grievances of his workers. First, the new foreman is carefully instructed how to identify bona fide grievances; then he is given an example of how a foreman antagonized his workers by becoming emotional:

The moral is, regardless of how the grievance is presented, and often it's done in a most uncomplimentary way, the supervisor has got to keep his head. . . . Putting a question to the man is usually a good way to meet a hot-headed approach. It snaps the man out of his mood, makes him

5 Harleigh Trecker, *Group Process in Administration* (New York: The Woman's Press, 1946), p. 210. (Parts of these quotes appear in italics in the original.)

31

think, and once you've got him thinking, even for a moment, he's bound to relax and cool off.[6]

Here we have a suggestion ("Put a question to the man!") which is clear and concrete enough to be useful to the foreman or personnel officer in handling an excited worker with a grievance. At the same time, a critical reader may wonder whether this recommendation is based on generalized knowledge. It is, after all, rather easy to think of a situation in which further questions (perhaps questions of less complementary or irrelevant kinds) would add fuel to the fire.

In short, books with rules of thumb may be useful to a practitioner because it is always helpful to listen to the experienced elders in one's field. However, the recommendations by some elders may be trivial, and some advice may well be misleading. What passes for accumulated working knowledge may, in part, be accumulated ignorance and malpractice that have obtained blessings as organizational policy and legitimate procedure. The reader of rules of thumb can never be sure whether he gets one or the other.

Descriptive Orientation

Many publications in social science are overviews of some social problem or problems. These publications

[6] Auren Uris, *Improved Foremanship* (New York: The Macmillan Company, 1948), pp. 114–115.

bring together the relevant facts in an orderly fashion. Most of them are written by academicians for college students, and they are used in what is typically a sophomore course in "social problems" or "social disorganization." These texts and courses are not designed to help students "solve" social problems, but rather to open the eyes of the students to the existence of these problems and to prepare the students for participation in democratic debate about them. Some of these works are written for more sophisticated audiences, but the purpose is the same: to bring together relevant facts without attempting to be particularly explicit on a practical level. Some will occasionally set forth scientific laws, for example, causes of crime, but most of the time they are plainly descriptive.

General descriptions of this kind are sometimes utilized by practitioners. Some working in the area of race relations, for example, report that the reading of Myrdal's *An American Dilemma* has been useful to them in their practice. Clearly, such a book cannot be used directly as a guide, say, for placing qualified Negroes in skilled trades, but the general insight into the pattern of discrimination given by such a book might help the practitioners in numerous subtle ways.

Of more immediate use to many practitioners are specific descriptions that indicate trends. Indicators of crime rates, or data on the quality of housing are meas-

33

ures of progress to those working in these fields. The uses of censuses and special surveys are numerous. A school superintendent uses them to estimate future enrollment and classroom needs. A leader of a settlement house, sensing a growing racial tension, secures the figures of influx of non-whites during the last decade in the census tract of his neighborhood. A YMCA secretary checks the income distribution of his town against the income of his clientele to see whether he provides an attractive enough program for the low-income residents.

Such descriptive knowledge is, of course, essential. One ought to know the facts before one leaps into action. However, even the most orderly and systematic collection of descriptive facts and trends does not give any specific advice on what action to take. At best it might indicate that some action is necessary, but it does not tell which one. To know what action is going to be effective, we need more than reliable, descriptive *facts*. We need reliable *laws* which say that if this and this is done, such and such an outcome is likely.

Application of Scientific Laws

In the literature of social practice we have read, scientific laws are hardly ever mentioned, and no explicit attempt is made to study their practical applications. To find illustrations of the use of scientific laws in social practice one has to go to fields that border on the biological sciences. Let us take an example from a book on the adjustment of the blind.[7]

Some blind persons have what traditionally has been called "a sixth sense." They can tell within inches the distance of a card put in front of their face, their distance from posts and trees, and some might even describe the shape of walls in front of them. One early attempt to explain this was furnished by Romains in 1924 who speculated that the nerve endings in the skin of the face can, with blindness, develop into little eyes, so that the skin actually comes to see. The phenomenon was called "facial vision." However, only a small proportion of blind people seem to acquire this sense for distance and obstacles to any great extent. Those who had acquired it were unable to tell how they did it, or exactly what processes were in operation. This posed a problem for the teachers in schools for the blind. They did not know how to teach an exceedingly useful skill to the blind.

In 1944 a series of experiments was published by a group of psychologists at Cornell University which shed new light on the phenomenon of "facial vision" and revealed it to be a process of "acoustic vision." The experiments were ingenious and simple. A number of subjects, some actually blind and others merely blindfolded,

7 Hector Chevigny and Sydell Braverman, *The Adjustment of the Blind* (Yale University Press: New Haven, 1950).

made a series of approaches to various obstacles under varied conditions. The subjects were also asked to estimate the distance of obstacles when they had been removed from the testing room and were provided with electronic equipment which transmitted the sounds made by experimenters approaching the same obstacles with microphones in their hands. It was assumed that if these estimates could be made accurately, only the sense of hearing was involved in the detection of objects by the blind. The results have been summarized as follows:

Each subject gave substantially the same estimates through perception by telephonic equipment as he had given in personal performance. "Facial vision," then, is a matter of experience and practice in the estimate of time in sound wave reflection. After long experience with blindness, the individual learns to determine, say, the distance of a card from his face in terms of inches, because of keenness of perception of the minute variations in length of sound bounce. The same principle works in the estimation of depth and space.[8]

Now, here was a scientific law: the longer time delay a person perceives in a sound reflection, the longer is the distance to the reflecting object. This discovery had practical implications.

Early efforts to teach the war-blinded to reorientate used the data of the Cornell tests. The work at Avon verified the

8 *Ibid.* p. 130.

Cornell findings by what amounted to clinical evidence. The use made of this new knowledge at Avon was simple. The newly blinded man, in the company of an instructor, approached certain objects while sharp sounds, usually those of a metal clicker, were produced. The instructor corrected mistakes in judgment of distance from objects, thus hastening the growth of hearing perception. It was found, not surprisingly, that capacities for grasping the idea of distance in terms of sound bounce varied greatly, but on the whole the results were such as to justify the view that further development in methods could cut the time of "learning to be blind" from a matter of years to weeks.[9]

The new law in the psychology of perception states that there is an equivalence between the distance a sound wave has traveled and the timing of its perceived sound bounce to the eardrums. This timing can, therefore, through simple laws of learning, be conditioned to conventional scales of distance. The recommendation to the practitioners teaching the blind thus becomes simple: let the blind person repeatedly practice the detection of reflection of sound waves; tell him when he estimates distances correctly and incorrectly; reward and encourage the more correct estimates! The success of this advice is measured by the fact that the time to learn to gauge distances was cut down "from a matter of years to weeks."

[9] *Ibid.* p. 130.

Such explicit usage of scientific laws for practical purposes is very rare in the practitioner literature.[10] One usually has to plow through hundreds of pages to find a single example. Yet it is obvious that *in order to give scientifically valid help to a client without conducting original research on his problem we must rely on scientific laws.* If we do not have any scientific laws, we do not have any scientific advice to offer. We might offer prudent help, wise help, even useful help, but to offer *scientific* advice we need to apply laws to the case. Judging from the scarcity of reliance on scientific laws in the practitioner literature, one might surmise that the practitioners of social science only rarely are able to offer genuine scientific advice. It seems a highly worthwhile task to improve upon this situation.

10 The suspicion that strict application of social theory is rare was voiced by Robert K. Merton in 1949: "Everyone who has read a textbook on scientific method knows the ideally constructed relations between scientific theory and applied research. Basic theory embraces key concepts (variables and constants), postulates, theorems and laws. Applied science consists simply in ascertaining (a) the variables relevant to the problem in hand, (b) the values of the variables and (c) in accordance with previous knowledge, setting forth the uniform relationships between these variables. It will be instructive to discover how often this ideal pattern actually occurs in the application of social science. We anticipate finding that it is the exceptional rather than the typical pattern." Merton proposes a research inquiry to account for the discrepancies and coincidences between the "ideal pattern" and the "actual pattern" of relations between basic and applied social science. See, Robert K. Merton, "The Role of Applied Social Science in the Formation of Policy: A Research Memorandum," *Philosophy of Science*, XVI (1949), pp. 161–181.

Three Fallacies in Current Literature for Practitioners

In the literature written for social practitioners there appear three fallacies that seem to enter into almost every discussion of how one can help practitioners of social science to use the research results of academic social science. The first fallacy is the common belief that one puts the social sciences to practical application simply by popularizing their content. Appalled by the abstractness of the academicians' formulations, the practitioner demands popular versions of the findings. However, it is not the act of popularization that is the crucial one in the applied fields. The handbook for chemical engineers is far from a popular version of chemistry. The crucial act here is to deduce a solution to a problem from a set of theoretical principles, and this has nothing to do with popularization. If anything, it requires very strict and technical formulations.

The second fallacy is more complex. It is assumed that the content of knowledge to be applied must match the content of the problem faced by the practitioner. Thus one assumes that the teacher in segregated schools can only be helped by research on desegregation, that the marriage counselor can only be helped by research on marital happiness and divorce, that the prison warden can only be aided by criminological and penological

39

research, et cetera. Of course, they normally are helped by such research; our contention is, however, that research knowledge with different content might be equally relevant to their problem.

Through interviews we collected information about a hundred different problems facing thirty practitioners in different lines of application of social science. The practitioners were simply asked to mention some typical problems that they encounter in the course of their practice. No claim is made that the problems mentioned are a representative cross-section of what occupies practitioners of social science. They at best give us an idea of the range of issues facing social practitioners. In looking over these problems it becomes clear that they do not fall into neatly specified areas that resemble the occupational titles of the practitioners. We find, for example, that the problems that most seriously preoccupy the prison warden are only to a minor extent those of rehabilitation and recidivism, although his job is publicly defined in those terms. Likewise, the problems of the head of a Scout camp are only to a minor extent the guidance of young people to a practice of Scouting ideals, although this is what the community defines as his role. Instead, the warden appears mostly preoccupied with the maintenance of good relations between the various departments of the prison—e.g., classification, custodial, and occupational training units—or

40

with the image of the prison in the mind of the public and the legislators. And the camp leader's most serious problems seem to be the recruitment, motivation, and morale of his camp counselors, and also the intricacies of camp-parent relations. All these issues are, of course, ultimately related to the official task of the practitioner. However, the point is that the day-by-day problems of the practitioners are of a different order and relate only indirectly to the literature on the manifest problems with which these practitioners deal, i.e., penology and adolescent education.

Thus it is a mistake to assume that the only knowledge that will help a practitioner is the academic knowledge about his publicly defined task. The discovery of this fallacy implies a moral of some significance. It is now obvious that the ones who want to feed more academic knowledge into applied practice are ill advised to work from library to practitioner's office, from knowledge about recognized problems to professionals or officials publicly designated to deal with them. The reverse must be the main approach: we must know the day-by-day issues facing the practitioner and then search the storehouse of academic knowledge to see whether it might aid him.

A third fallacy is found in the idea that the number of social problems is, if not indefinite, at least very large. This does not seem to be the case. Although there is an

41

immense complexity of symptoms and innumerable combinations of them, the number of diseases seems reasonably finite and limited. In popular opinion, the marriage counselor, the college admissions officer, the prison warden, the vocational guidance adviser, the personnel manager, the settlement house worker, deal with widely different problems. However, a close analysis suggests that there is an amazing overlap of problems, once these are phrased in more general terms. The group worker tries to prevent a street corner society from developing criminal practices; the prison warden tries to prevent the emergence of subgroups of internees and guards with corrupt patterns. Both are basically facing the same problem: how to prevent the emergence of a deviant subculture. The settlement house director needs to motivate volunteers to act as group leaders; the camp counselor has to motivate children to participate in new endeavors and games; the personnel director has to persuade a worker to take on a less attractive replacement for some period of time. All basically face the same problem: how to motivate persons to take on a new position. The fund-raiser for a social agency must persuade people who have already contributed to charity to give his organization further support; a librarian must change the ideas of what constitutes sufficient reading from a few books every year to a few books per month; the advertising manager for a men's shoe industry must change the American male's notion that it is sufficient to have only two or three pairs of shoes in his closet to the belief that half a dozen or more are necessary; the public health nurse must change the impression of children that it is enough to brush one's teeth once a day to a conviction that it must be done three times a day. All these practitioners really face the same problem: how to redefine what constitutes compliance with a social norm.

And so, one can continue to show that where common sense sees different problems, scientific theory sees the same problem. This is an extremely comforting idea. It implies that if we can find scientific solutions to a small number of *theoretical problems* we really have solutions for a large number of practical issues.

However, current social practice is many steps removed from any such possibility. Social practitioners are not aware of any social theory that can provide this service. They are apt to say that the knowledge available in social science is not developed enough to be used in this way.

A Random List of Books and Articles Suggested as Helpful by Practitioners

Abrams, Charles. *The Future of Housing*. New York and London: Harper and Bros., 1946.

43

Allport, Gordon W. *The Nature of Prejudice*. Cambridge, Mass.: Addison-Wesley Pub. Company, 1954.

Auer, J. J., and H. L. Eubank. *Handbook for Discussion Readers*. Harper and Bros., 1954.

Case Reports in Public Administration. Social Science Research Council, Committee on Public Administration, Special Committee on Research Materials, 1940.

Cassidy, Rosalind, Hilda Clute Kozman, and Margaret Mead. *Counseling Girls in a Changing Society: A Guide for Counselors and Teachers in High School and College*. New York and London: McGraw-Hill Book Company, Inc., 1947.

Chevigny, Hector, and Sydell Braverman. *The Adjustment of the Blind*. New Haven: Yale University Press, 1950.

Clark, Kenneth B. "Desegregation and Appraisal of Evidence," *Journal of Social Issues*, 9, 4 (1953).

——. *Prejudice and Your Child*. Boston: The Beacon Press, 1955.

Coyle, Grace. *Group Work with American Youth*. Harper and Bros., 1948.

Crawford, P. L., D. I. Melamud, and J. R. Dampson. *Working with Teen-age Gangs*. Report on the Central Harlem Street Clubs Project, New York City Welfare Council, 1950.

Cuber, John F. *Marriage Counseling Practice*. New York: Appleton-Century-Crofts Co., 1948.

Cutsforth, Thomas D. *The Blind in School and Society*. New York: Appleton-Century, Inc., 1934.

Dressler, David. *Probation and Parole*. New York: Columbia University Press, 1951.

Fellows, Margaret M., and Stella A. Koenig. *How to Raise Funds by Mail*. New York: McGraw-Hill, 1950.

Fox, Lionel W. *The English Prison and Borstal Systems*. London: Routledge and Kegan Paul, 1952.

Freud, Anna. *The Ego and Its Mechanisms of Defense*. London: The Hogarth Press and the Institute of Psychoanalysis, 1948.

Garvian, Ruth. *Understanding Juvenile Delinquency*. New York: Oxford Book Company, 1954.

Geiger, Jacob C. *Health Officers' Manual: General Information Regarding the Administration and Technical Problems of the Health Officer*. Philadelphia and London: W. B. Saunders Company, 1939.

Green, Sidney L. and Allan B. Rotherberg. *A Manual of First Aid for Mental Health*. New York: Julian Press, 1953.

Hamman, Bert. *Physical Capacities and Job Placement*. Stockholm: Nordisk Rotogravyr, 1951.

Harms, Ernest. *Handbook of Child Guidance*. New York: Child Care Publications, 1947.

Hymes, James L. *Discipline*. New York: Bureau of Publications, Teachers College, Columbia University, 1951.

Johns, Ray. *Executive Responsibility: An Analysis of Executive Responsibilities in the Work of Voluntary Community Social Welfare Organizations*. New York: Association Press, 1954.

Juran, Joseph M., and N. N. Barish. *Case Studies in Industrial Management*. New York, Toronto, London: McGraw-Hill Company, 1955.

Lee, Irving J. *How to Talk with People: a Program for Preventing Troubles that Come When People Talk Together*. New York: Harper and Bros., 1952.

Levy, Harold P. *Building a Popular Movement*. New York: Russell Sage Foundation, 1944.

Mee, John F., editor. *Personnel Handbook*. New York: The Ronald Press, 1951.

Mills, C. Wright, Clarence Senior, and Rose K. Goldsen. *The Puerto Rican Journey: New York's Newest Migrants*. New York: Harper and Bros., 1950.

Mudd, Emily. *The Practice of Marriage Counseling*. New York: Association Press, 1951.

Murray, Janet P., and E. Clyde. *Guide-Lines to Group Leaders*. New York: Whiteside Inc. and William Morrow and Company, Inc., 1954.

Myrdal, Gunnar, with the assistance of Richard Sterner and Arnold Rose. *An American Dilemma: The Negro Problem and Modern Democracy*. New York: Harper and Bros., 1944.

Pepinsky, Harold B., and Paulina N. Pepinsky. *Counseling Theory and Practice*. New York: The Ronald Press, 1954.

Reckless, Walter C. *The Etiology of Delinquent and Criminal Behavior*. Social Science Research Council Bulletin 50, 1943.

Rogers, Carl. *Psychotherapy and Personality Change*. Chicago: University of Chicago Press, 1954.

Sorenson, Roy, and Hedley S. Dimock. *Designing Education in Values: A Case Study in Institutional Change*. New York: Association Press, 1955.

Stein, Harold, editor. *Public Administration and Policy Development*. New York: Harcourt Brace, 1952.

45

Tappan, Paul, editor. *Contemporary Correction.* New York, Toronto, London: McGraw-Hill Book Company, Inc., 1951.

Teamwork in Our Town. Pamphlet by Community Chests and Councils of America, Inc., n.d.

Toward Solving the Puzzle. Pamphlet of Massachusetts Community Organization Service, n.d.

Tucker, Henleigh B. *Group Processes in Administration.* New York: The Woman's Press, 1945.

Uris, Auren. *Improved Foremanship.* New York: The Macmillan Company, 1948.

Viteles, Morris S. *Motivation and Morale in Industry.* New York: W. W. Norton and Company, Inc., 1953.

Warren, Roland L. *Studying Your Community.* Russell Sage Foundation, New York, 1955.

Weaver, Robert C. *The Negro Ghetto.* New York: Harcourt Brace, 1948.

Whyte, William Foote. *Street Corner Society: The Social Structure of an Italian Slum.* Chicago: The University of Chicago Press, 1952.

Wiles, Kimball. *Supervision for Better Schools: The Role of the Official Leader in Program Development.* New York: Prentice-Hall, 1950.

Wilson, Gertrude, and Grace Ryland. *Social Work Group Practice.* Boston: Houghton Mifflin Company, 1949.

Winsley, Edith. *The Community and Public Health Nursing: a Handbook for and About Boards and Citizens' Committees.* New York: The Macmillan Company, 1950.

Wittenberg, Rudolph. *So You Want to Help People: a Mental Hygiene Primer for Group Leaders.* New York: Association Press, 1947.

Woodward, C. Vann. *The Strange Case of Jim Crow: a Brief Account of Segregation.* New York: Oxford University Press, 1955.

3 The Knowledge of Social Theorists

Sociologists, of course, know a large number of facts about their society—how many Negroes there are, how many people belong to voluntary associations, how many persons have advanced into high-ranking jobs, and other facts reported in *A Sociological Almanac for the United States* and similar publications. But, apart from such facts, are there in the body of sociological knowledge any laws (or law-like propositions) that can be called confirmed or trustworthy?

The answer is undoubtedly "Yes." However, the actual number of sociological laws is subject to debate, because different sociologists cannot agree on how stiff to make criteria in calling a general statement about societal life a sociological law. Furthermore, there is a lack of agreement about the precise language and formulation of these laws. A survey of the laws in theoretical sociology becomes, therefore, subject to some convictions and preferences not shared by colleagues in all details.

With this caveat I shall review in this chapter the laws of sociology that I have found most useful.[1] In the following text some of the more important laws are indented, and some of the most important 'terms' used in their formulation are put within single quotation marks at the spots in the text where they have been defined, or where they are introduced as undefined primitives to be used in the definitions of the other terms. (Theories are made of terms and laws, and this simple typographical convention keeps them separate.) Let us begin by surveying some key terms in the technical language used in sociology.

---

1 Some of these laws are well supported by research and command great confidence. Others are supported by weaker evidence and often developed within a "humanistic" rather than a "scientific" tradition of social thought. Many of these laws are logically related, that is, some can be deduced from combinations of other laws and technical terms. A further treatise about sociological laws that reviews and evaluates evidence and spells out interrelations between laws is much needed in the sociological literature. So far this is only available for micro-sociology in George C. Homans, *Social Behavior: Its Elementary Forms* (New York: Harcourt Brace & World, 1961).

48

SOCIOLOGICAL TERMS

Nothing I know of can change the fact that sociological terminology appears tedious and arbitrary. Nevertheless, it is not altogether pointless to be concerned with it; among other things, an orderly terminology will, in the end, help us formulate laws and arrive at conclusions that are far from tedious and arbitrary. My personal preference is for technical terms with incipient similarities to everyday language. Use of such terms, rather than the novel or foreign ones favored by some sociologists, makes it possible for laymen to achieve a fair understanding of sociology without learning the details of its technical language.[2]

Types of Actions

Wherever and whenever human actions occur, some of these are *'communicative actions'* [3] (ideas, symbolic acts,

2 The reader may test this assumption by skipping the next twenty-four pages and turning to "Sociological Laws" on p. 73.
3 The seven terms appearing in italics are "basic" in the sense that combined with each other and with terms from other sciences and logical terms they render nominal definitions of the other terms used in this essay. The literature of sociology has several alternative lists of basic terms. One such list known as the "means-end schema" was obtained by Talcott Parsons from a review of some major European contributions to sociology; see his *The Structure of Social Action* (New York: McGraw-Hill, 1937, pp. 44–45). Later Parsons revised and elab-

communications) and some are, for want of a more descriptive term, simply *'physical actions'* (manual actions). The communicative actions are the most interesting: Through speech, dance, writing, drawing, and the like, men tell each other what they have seen, heard, or felt; what they want and what they do not want. They constitute social reality and they determine the way we find the structure of physical reality.[4]

Some communications are *'descriptions,'* for example: "He is an M.D."; "This is a paper in sociology." Others are *'evaluations,'* for example: "He is a good doctor";

---

orated this list of basic terms and arrived at a new set of "fundamental concepts" called "The Frame of Reference of the Theory of Action." See Talcott Parsons and Edward A. Shils, *Toward a General Theory of Action* (Cambridge, Mass.: Harvard University Press, 1952), pp. 4–8.

[4] Cf. Torgny T. Segerstedt, *Verklighet och värde* (Lund, Sweden: C. K. V. Gleerup, 1938). Segerstedt's analysis of symbols and reality seems to me to be the soundest basis for a theoretical sociology. It avoids the implicit assumptions about sociological data found in sociological thinking using a language borrowed from the physical sciences (i.e., any mechanistic approach such as the group dynamics school) or the biological sciences (e.g., the functionalist school), while it retains and makes use of the powerful methods in manipulating and processing the same data that have been developed in the biological and physical sciences. The emphasis on symbols in theoretical sociology makes it natural to phrase sociological discourse in the language of dramatics. Simple dramatic models of social intercourse (e.g., role theory) have long been available, and more complicated ones are emerging; see, for example, Hugh Dalziel Duncan, *Communication and Social Order* (New York: The Bedminster Press, 1962). The ease of discussing sociological events in a dramatic language is, however, hampered by some difficulties of relating the current language of social research to the language of drama.

"This is a difficult paper." Still others are *'prescriptions,'* for example: "See your doctor!"; "Read this paper!" Often, to classify a communication, we have to know something about the situation in which it occurs. Given such knowledge, it is usually possible to place any communicative action in one of these three categories. If we say "It is raining," we may actually communicate "It is now raining" (description); "The weather is bad" (evaluation); or "Shut the window!" (prescription).

A different classification of human actions is based on a fundamental fact of biology: human beings, like other vertebrates, have a central (cerebrospinal) and a peripheral (autonomic) nervous system, the former controlling primarily the skeletal muscles, the latter controlling primarily the smooth muscles and the glands. In common parlance, the duality is reflected by the distinction between head and heart, and between skill and emotion. In psychological theories of learning, the distinction reappears as one between response and reinforcement. In sociological theory the distinction has been approximated by Weber's separation of rational and traditional actions from affective ones.[5] I shall ex-

[5] Max Weber, *Wirtschaft und Gesellschaft,* 3d ed. (Tübingen: J. C. B. Mohr, 1947), p. 12. In the current terminology advocated by Parsons and others this separation reappears as a differentiation between "instrumental" and "expressive" actions. Parsons' distinction, however, is based on a teleological consideration: instrumental actions are means to reach some gratifying goal, while expressive ones are gratifying in themselves. I would like to avoid, for the present, such considerations.

51

press this dichotomy in terms of *'executive actions'* (e.g., driving a car, giving a scientific lecture, getting dressed for a football game) as opposed to *'emotive actions'* (e.g., hand wringing, reading romantic poetry, cheering a team's victory in a football game). The distinction is, of course, an analytic one: almost every concrete behavior contains both executive and emotive components. In any sociological analysis of rhetoric and art, ideology and religion, this separation of executive and emotive components seems crucial. When we say with Shakespeare that "All the world's a stage" (an emotive description), this is distinct from an executive description such as "There is a routine in real life, each man going through a prearranged course"; or, "There is a good deal of trivial make-believe in each man's conduct." [6] Art, religion, and ethics differ from science, economy, and jurisprudence in their abundance of expressive actions.

The division of actions into executive and emotive cuts across the previous classification of actions into communicative and physical, also the subdivision of communications into descriptions, evaluations, and prescriptions. Thus, we have executive physical actions

---

It is also important to keep the distinction between the executive and the emotive separate from Sorokin's distinction between the ideational and the sensate, which will be mentioned later (p. 66).

6 *Cf.* Charles L. Stevenson, *Ethics and Language* (New Haven: Yale University Press, 1944), pp. 73–74.

(e.g., batting a baseball) and emotive physical actions (e.g., the grimace and the flinging down of the bat by a player who misses a ball). We have executive communications and emotive communications, and these are further divisible into descriptions, evaluations, and prescriptions.

By way of example, not as definitions, some familiar actions are listed below in accordance with this classification:

Manual work: e.g., painting of walls	Executive physical action
White-collar work: e.g., proof-reading, shorthand	Executive communications
Ceremonial activities: e.g., handshakes, parades	Emotive physical actions
Spiritual activities: e.g., prayers, art viewing	Emotive communications
Scientific discourse: e.g., statements of definitions, laws, accounts of experimental apparatus	Executive descriptions
Economic discourse: e.g., prices, wages, fees	Executive evaluations
Governmental discourse: e.g., laws, orders, decisions	Executive prescriptions
Artistic presentations: e.g., paintings, sculpture, poetry	Emotive descriptions
Religious language: e.g., statements about sin, salvation, and the after-life	Emotive evaluations

| Ethical language: e.g., exhortations about charity or uprightness | Emotive prescriptions |

The ability to manipulate communications—combining them into new ideas, adjusting them to new situations, relating them to themes—varies, of course, from individual to individual, depending on heredity and training; it constitutes what in a broad sense is called intelligence. Intelligence, it hardly needs to be said, enters into many sociological problems; a case in point is the long controversy about the role of the genius in history. While it is possible to make general conclusions about the intelligence level of various social classes, sociology, however scientific, cannot be credited with the ability to predict the action of high intelligences accurately—unless we make the flattering but unrealistic assumption that the sociologist can predict all intelligent actions in advance. This is one of the elements of uncertainty inherent in all sociological forecasts, and it should be remembered particularly by those who attempt to apply sociology to achieve practical results.

Positions

A routine answer to the question "Who is Mr. X?" begins with a list of his past and present positions. When they are speaking generally, sociologists use the term position (or status) to include every capacity in which an individual can be expected to act. There are several ways of identifying a position; the one I prefer makes use of the wording of prescriptions. Typically, the grammatical subject of a prescription is a word that defines position; whatever subject modifies a prescription is a 'position.'

Students	shall go to class
Gentlemen	are requested to wear jackets in the dining room
Drivers	should proceed carefully

The names at the left are subjects in prescriptions, and each one thus defines a position.

Much effort has been applied to the task of grouping positions in large categories; for example, the different evaluation (e.g., prestige) given to positions assigns them to different 'ranks.' Beyond this, however, no generally accepted way of classifying positions has been found.[7] It is natural, however, to classify them according to the bases used for describing the occupant: a characteristic of the person himself (male, genius, invalid) or his characteristic relation to other occupants of positions (mother, customer, guest), or his relation to a super-unit (citizen, subscriber, member).

[7] For a sophisticated approach, see S. F. Nadel, *The Theory of Social Structure* (Glencoe, Ill.: The Free Press, 1957), ch. 2.

Cross-cutting this classification is one that designates positions in accordance with the degree to which they are based on stable characteristics of the occupant; this classification is carried out in terms of 'ascription,' [8] For example, racial positions deriving from a basically unchangeable characteristic such as skin color are marked by a high degree of ascription; so are positions deriving from kinship and from membership in religious, national, and other units difficult for anyone to leave [9]

---

[8] *Cf.* Ralph Linton, *Study of Man* (New York: Appleton-Century, 1936), pp. 115 ff.

[9] The following summary chart may be helpful in grasping the two bases for classification of positions we have discussed so far:

	High stability of the characteristic used as a basis for designation	*Low stability of the characteristic used as a basis for designation*
Designation of position in terms of a *sub-unit of the position* (e.g., characteristic of occupant himself).	Negro	Sick
Designation of position in terms of its *relation to other positions*.	Son	Customer
Designation of position in terms of its relation to a *super-unit of positions*.	Citizen	Subscriber
	High ascription	Low ascription

Later (page 68), we will develop another classification in terms of institutional realms and the ways in which institutional values are created, transmitted, and received.

Social Relations

To identify a 'social relation' (or social role),[10] we mention two positions and hyphenate them: parent-child is one social relation, student-teacher is another, customer-dealer a third, and so on almost ad infinitum. Technically speaking, two positions define a social relation if the prescriptions addressed to one contain references to the other: "Children should obey their parents"; "Parents should guide their children." Occupants of the two positions which constitute a social relation are referred to as 'associates' and the prescriptions involved are 'role prescriptions.' It is often useful to indicate which social relations a person can enter into by virtue of occupying a given position (e.g., student-professor, student-student, student-dean) and who are his associates in any social relation. Information in these areas constitutes a further routine answer to the question, "Who is Mr. X?"

Since social relations are even more numerous than positions, the need to classify them in some orderly way

---

10 The term 'social role' has a large number of meanings in sociology, and it might be wise to return to the common-sense notion 'social relation.' A technical definition of the latter (*soziale Beziehung*) was furnished by Max Weber (*op. cit.,* p. 13).

has been felt by many sociologists. Perhaps the simplest classification is in terms of the time span of such a relation: some are 'lasting,' like a marriage; some are not, like a flirtation; some are 'sporadic,' like voting every fourth year for the president; and some, like housework, never end.

More complex classifications can also be made. For example, a social relation is termed 'contingent' to the extent that the position (and rank) in which a person enters can be altered by the actions of his associates.[11] It is clear that some relations, for instance, those involving ascribed positions, have practically zero contingency; for example, in a man-woman or an adult-child relation nothing the man, or the adult, does can alter the fact that his associate is a woman, or a child. Likewise, a relation between two doctors has fairly low contingency; virtually nothing one doctor does can revoke the doctorate held by the other. Many relations have a one-way contingency; to illustrate, in a professor-student relation the student's status is in the hands of the professor, since the latter has the authority to flunk him out of school, but it is virtually impossible for the student to force the professor to give up his chair. Still other relations are completely contingent; for example, the buyer-seller re-

11 Most discussions of what I have called "contingent relations" are found under the topic of "ascription" in sociological textbooks and treatises. However, ascription is an attribute of positions, not social relations, and a new term may be needed here.

lation is contingent on the price, credit, and delivery conditions.

A further measure applied to any social relation indicates its degree of familiarity: any relation of an individual is 'familiar' to the extent that his associates can describe and evaluate his past and present actions. In simple words, very familiar social relations are those in which the participants have little privacy: they know almost everything about each other. There are also social relations that are one-sidedly familiar; an instance is the psychiatrist-patient role, in which one party knows a great deal about the life of the other but the reverse is not true. Many urban social relations have a very low degree of familiarity; our landlords, merchants, bosses generally know little about our life.

A related measure is the extent to which a social relation is specialized or not. Here the criterion is not how much our associate knows about us, but how much we actually do together. The greater the proportion of all our action that enters a social relation, the less 'specialized' it is. A young brother and sister do most everything together and have little specialization in their relation; as they grow older they do more and more with other people and relatively less with each other. Their relation becomes more specialized but may, of course, remain familiar.

Finally, we measure social relations in terms of how

impersonal they are. A relation is most 'impersonal' when the prescriptions governing one associate are the same no matter who occupies the position. Modern occupational roles are very impersonal; a salesgirl is supposed to treat all customers alike. Family relations are not at all impersonal: The wife treats her own husband differently from the way she treats other husbands.

It may be useful to group certain of these attributes of social relations together into two gross clusters. Some of our social relations are associations with 'strangers'; that is, persons with whom we have less lasting, more sporadic, less familiar, more specialized, and more impersonal relations. Other of our social relations are associations with 'neighbors'; that is persons with whom we have more lasting, less sporadic, more familiar, less specialized, and less impersonal relations. This manifold scale from neighbor to stranger is useful when we want to separate the medieval from the modern, the rural from the urban, and the familistic from the bureaucratic.[12] While other combinations of the attributes

[12] For the first systematic use of the general distinction between neighbor and stranger and some related notions, see Ferdinand Tonnies, *Gemeinschaft und Gesellschaft* (Leipzig: Fues Verlag, 1887). A systematic analysis of the content of this in other types of social relations was made in 1941 by Pitirim A. Sorokin. See his *Social and Cultural Dynamics* (New York: The Bedminster Press, 1962), vol. IV, pp. 5–41. See also the so-called pattern variable schema developed by Talcott Parsons and Edward A. Shils, "Values, Motives, and Systems of Action," in *Toward a General Theory of Action*, ed. by Parsons and Shils (Cambridge, Mass.: Harvard University Press, 1952), pp. 76–88.

of social relations are possible,[13] this particular cluster-
ing is the only one for which we have a theoretical explanation (*supra,* pp. 78–80).

Organizations and Markets

Certain positions require the occupant to issue prescriptions and his associates to obey them. These are actually
legion: the judge issuing court orders, the parent direct-
ing his children, the boss giving directives. These positions we may call 'leaderships,' recognizing, of course,
that what is commonly meant by leadership may involve
more than the license to issue prescriptions.

An 'organization' is defined as a set of social relations
whose role prescriptions are issued from a common
leadership. All the associates in an organization form a
social 'group.' The Smith family and the Brown family
are virtually identical organizations—both include hus-

[13] Combinations may be illustrated in summary tabulations:

	More contingent	*Less contingent*
More familiar		
More Impersonal	Psychiatrist-Patient	Priest-Parishioner
Less Impersonal	Fiancé-Fiancée	Husband-Wife
Less intimate		
More Impersonal	Salesman-Customer	Young-Old
Less Impersonal	Parent-Teacher	Nephew-Uncle

band-wife, father-son, father-daughter, mother-son, mother-daughter, brother-sister, brother-brother, and sister-sister relations, with the leadership of the mother and the father—but they form two separate groups because the leaders, Mr. and Mrs. Smith in the one instance and Mr. and Mrs. Brown in the other, are different. The distinction between organization and group emphasizes the fact that many separate groups can have the same organization. In complex organizations we often find positions whose occupants exercise some discretion in issuing prescriptions, and we can identify subdivisions of an organization by identifying the social relations over which they exercise such discretion.

Where there is no central leadership at all in social relations, we deal no longer with an organization. Social relations that are not subject to control by a common leadership constitute a 'market.' An invisible hand in the form of special social mechanisms, but no central authority, directs what shall go on when buyers and sellers meet; when political candidates encounter their constituents; when a young man meets a young woman; when a scientist presents his findings to another scientist. Of course, such encounters are by no means normless; a body of shared prescriptions regulates them. However, these prescriptions merely set up a framework within which exchanges take place; they do not determine the outcome of the exchanges.

In the many markets found in any population the air is full of tempting calls: "Buy," "Join," "Come," "Give," "See," "Try," "Go" and so forth. Technically these 'market calls' are also prescriptions, but they differ from organizational prescriptions in that no one is punished for avoiding them, and there is no necessary reward for obeying them. A market call designates an 'offering' in the market place: merchandise, ideas, services, opportunities to do something. When such a call is actually followed, that is, when such a prescription is obeyed, we have a 'market response.'

To designate the participants in a market we need a special term (since market is defined independently of the persons who enact it), and that is—'public.' It is publics that trade on the stock market; publics that vote in elections; publics of young men and women that enter the marriage market; and publics that write and read scientific books and journals.

Markets and organizations have complex interrelations. Within the framework of any large decentralized organization one may find islands that are markets. Contrariwise, smaller organizations participating in a market dominated by one large organization may tend to become, in effect, subdivisions of the large organization. While the distinction between organization and market is clear in theory, it is often difficult to draw the line between them in practice.

Any market or organization can be related to any other through a variety of means. The simplest are: (1) 'outside (out-group) relations,' that is, social relations between associates whose positions are in different markets or organizations, (2) 'overlapping memberships,' that is, persons having positions in more than one market or organization at the same time, and (3) 'mobility,' that is, movements of persons from positions in one market or organization to positions in another in the course of time. These three phenomena tie the markets and organizations of a society together in an intricate fashion, and are usually very rewarding objects of sociological study.

Sociologists often focus their attention on the ways in which a given organization or market relates to others. They are, therefore, apt to become specialists, not so much in the "inside story," the internal workings of any organization or market, but in their "outside story," that is, how they relate to other organizations and markets.

Themes

The huge number of actions that enter into any sociological inquiry, particularly a macrosociological one, make it an essential task to select a small number of actions that can, in a sense, summarize all the actions involved. In any set of communicative actions some will be found to be generating ideas of which other symbolic expressions in the set are more or less clear implications, or generated ideas, according to the means (e.g., grammar and syntax) available for the manipulation of symbols. I shall call the generating communications 'themes.' Almost every society seems to have some descriptive themes about the nature of man and the universe. Scientific laws have become the descriptive themes of modern Western culture ever since Newton's laws of gravity and Darwin's principles of evolution replaced the theological themes of providence and creation. Evaluative themes stating that man is good or bad, and that the welfare of social organization is more important or less important than the welfare of individuals, also run through the history of many societies. Prescriptive themes, too, are easy to illustrate; the notion that people should be treated as equals, regardless of sex, race, or religion, is a currently potent prescriptive theme. Such themes serve to sum up the vast number of day-to-day descriptions, evaluations, and prescriptions and, thus, provide convenient bases for gross characterizations of sociological subject matter.

There is great variation in the extent to which such themes can account for all communicative actions occurring in a social unit, that is, in the extent to which the social unit is 'rational' or 'pragmatic.' In the rational social unit every communication in use is implied in existing themes; in the pragmatic unit new ideas bear no explicit relation to past ideas, but presumably emerge from trial and error.

Integration of culture into themes appears to be the exception rather than the rule. Sorokin's studies make it apparent that most communicative actions in most times and places remain 'congeries', that is, relatively unrelated to each other. A more universally applicable gross characterization of a multitude of communicative actions can, however, be made by taking notice of how closely they refer to sense data, that is, occurrences which are directly presented to the human senses. When the overwhelming number of communications refer directly to sense data, they are called 'sensate'; when they are remote from material and biological events impinging directly on our senses, they are called 'ideational.' This continuum from sensate to ideational has been proposed by Sorokin, who proved its worth in his impressive enterprise to characterize various phases of our civilization.[14] Our own time, of course, is very sensate.

Institutional Realms and Their Stratification

A different, and more certain, answer to the sociologist's need for concepts that condense large numbers of ac-

14 Sorokin, *op. cit.*, vol. 1, pp. 66–101.

tions is represented by what I shall call 'institutional values.' These—knowledge, prosperity, order, beauty, sacredness, virtue—are defined by pooling all communications of a given kind which are consonant with each other. By consonant communications we mean those that are not in contradiction or discord in the light of the norms for their manipulation regardless of whether they constitute themes or not.[15]

Thus, the sum total of consonant executive descriptions in a set of communications we call 'knowledge'; this would not include circumstances for which no descriptions exist in the set, nor descriptions felt to be in contradiction. We define the sum total of all executive evaluations in a set as 'prosperity.' Prosperity is thus constituted by the net worth of things (e.g., goods or resources); persons (e.g., income earners); actions (e.g., services). It is important to observe that it is not the things, persons, or actions that constitute prosperity but the net evaluation of them, just as knowledge is not a collection of things, persons, or actions but a description of them. The executive prescriptions that are consonant with each other add up to what we call 'order.' Laws, ordinances, executive orders, decisions, rules, policies, programs, understandings, commands and traditions are some of the names we give to the executive

---

[15] Leon Festinger, *A Theory of Cognitive Dissonance* (Evanston, Ill.: Row Peterson, 1957), pp. 12–15.

prescriptions that constitute the social and political order. Emotive descriptions in consonance constitute what we know as 'beauty'; emotionally engaging symbolism in esthetic balance belongs here. Emotive evaluations in consonance, for instance, adoration and reverence, constitute 'sacredness.' Finally, emotive prescriptions in consonance constitute 'virtue'; the consistent and emotionally engaging prescriptions of charity, prudence, fortitude, temperance, and justice belong here.

Each institutional value has its 'creators,' 'purveyors,' and 'receivers.' Thus, new knowledge is produced by scholars, transmitted by teachers and received by students. Persons who produce modifications in the social order are rulers; those who apply or transmit their prescriptions are administrators; and those who are at the receiving end are the subjects. The creator of prosperity is a producer (earner); the recipient is a consumer (spender); and the transmitter is known as a dealer. Here we have, in effect, an additional classification of positions.[16] Of course, one person or organization

16 This classification may be summarized as follows:

Institutional Realms and Institutional Values	Creators	Purveyors	Receivers
Science (knowledge)	Scholars	Teachers	Students
Economy (prosperity)	Producers	Dealers	Consumers

may at times appear in all these capacities simultaneously.

An 'institutional realm' consists of the positions (in organizations and markets) that produce, transmit, and receive a single institutional value. Thus, the organizations and markets involved in the creation, transmission, and reception of knowledge constitute 'science'; those concerned with order constitute the 'polity'; those concerned with prosperity make up the 'economy.' The institutional realm of art comprises the organizations and markets that produce, purvey, and receive beauty; the realm of 'religion' stands in the same relation to the sacred, and the realm of 'ethics' to virtue. Most organizations and markets participate in several institutional realms, but in general each organization or market is engaged primarily in one or two realms.

The share of an institutional value produced, transmitted, or received by a person, group, or public defines the place of this person, group, or public in the 'strata'

Polity (order)	Rulers	Administrators	Subjects
Art (beauty)	Artists	[Performers *]	[Art public *]
Religion (sacredness)	Prophets	Clergymen	Laymen
Ethics (virtue)	["Fountains of morals" *]	Moralists	["Men who hear virtue's call" *]

* No all-inclusive noun seems available in the English language.

of the institutional realm. Each institutional realm has its typical mode of stratification. We may say that command of knowledge defines 'competence,' control of social order defines 'power,' command of prosperity defines 'riches'; likewise, command of beauty indicates 'taste,' command of the sacred indicates 'holiness,' and command of virtue indicates moral 'rectitude.' This multi-faceted approach to social stratification we shall soon find very useful; however, for the time being, let us simply take note of the fact that money and power are not everything that enters the stratification of men. Stratification in terms of knowledge is becoming increasingly predominant in modern societies, as seen, for example, in the emphasis on formal education. Stratification based on religious criteria (holiness), has played an enormous part in many civilizations, and is still very much in presence in many non-Western societies.

More could be said about the various terms we need to talk about stratification systems. For example, the notion 'elite' is used to designate those who command the highest shares of any institutional value. Also, the term 'caste' is often used by sociologists to denote an ascribed stratum, that is, one in which no member is allowed to leave, neither through economic, political, or educational advancement, nor other forms of mobility such as intermarriage with higher strata. However, ascription is always a matter of degree, and one is well

70

advised to speak about more or less caste-like situations, rather than castes and open strata. For example, one may say that the situation of the American Negro during the present trend toward desegregation is becoming less caste-like. Other terms in the field of social stratification such as class consciousness and class struggles will be dealt with in a later context (*infra*, pp. 120–121).

By Way of Summary

If we list the most important terms we have discussed we will notice that they fall into an orderly schema, from the simplest to the most inclusive. An outline of the schema is shown in the adjoining tabulation; it can easily be amended to include the categories of creators, purveyors, and receivers in each realm, and the different designations of organizations and markets within each realm.

INSTITUTIONAL REALMS, VALUES, AND STRATIFICATIONS

Basic Action Type	Institutional Value	Mode of Stratification	Institutional Realm
Executive			
Description	Knowledge	Competence	Science
Evaluation	Prosperity	Riches	Economy
Prescription	Order	Power	Polity
Emotive			
Description	Beauty	Taste	Art
Evaluation	Sacredness	Holiness	Religion
Prescription	Virtue	Rectitude	Ethics

Such a schema reveals the simplicity in the way any society is composed.

A rule of thumb in the analysis of any society is that events in one institutional realm of a society can (and usually do) have consequences in other institutional realms. This rule seems to be the *sense moral* of the sociological tradition; certainly most classics of sociology achieved their fame through detailed accounts of institutional interdependencies. Thus, Plato's *Republic* is full of analyses of the interdependence of institutional realms and resultant recommendations for organizing the relations between them, particularly between science and polity. In reading Machiavelli we are rewarded by analyses of the relations between polity, economy, and religion. Reading Marx today, we still take an interest in his analysis of the relations between economy and polity, though we consider obsolete most of his thinking on the internal workings of the economy. In Max Weber's study of the Protestant ethic, the focus is on the consequences that events in religion have for events in the economy. In Durkheim's analysis of primitive religion, the focus is on the interdependence of religion and other institutions in society. Thus an amazing amount of what, by reasonable consensus, is called worthwhile in sociology has had precisely this focus: How do events in one institutional realm, in planned or unplanned ways, affect events in another institutional

72

realm? Needless to say, these are exceedingly complex topics even to treat descriptively.[17]

SOCIOLOGICAL LAWS

The terms we have reviewed, like other technical vocabularies, can be used as identification badges for professionals who belong to the same field, and they can also be used to impress outsiders. They also may serve as a kind of "shopping list" for the sociologist who wants to give a descriptive account of a society, an institutional realm, a market, an organization, a relation or a position, by telling him what to look for in the vast array of scattered details that confronts him in such a task. The terms thus tell what is "sociologically relevant." However, they are important for a very different reason: The terms are used in the formulation of sociological laws, the information-packed sentences that sum up what we know about social life. The balance of this chapter will be devoted primarily to a sampling of such laws.

[17] The most successful attempt to deal with them is perhaps the well-known study of Middletown in the twenties and thirties: Robert S. Lynd and Helen M. Lynd, *Middletown* (New York: Harcourt Brace, 1929); *Middletown in Transition* (New York: Harcourt Brace, 1937).

On the Limits of Action

The simplest law of sociology is the principle of the limit of actions—

> The number of possible actions per person is limited.

That everybody has had some experience with this principle is clear from the amount of complaining we do about lack of time and energy. We all know too well that one cannot be completely involved in, say, science and also in politics, money making, or the raising of a big family. The principle of the limit of actions is most applicable to large groups or to total societies, where individual idiosyncrasies do not disturb the overall trends. It suggests, for example, that a low birth rate, that is, fewer children to bring up, releases actions for engagement by other institutions and, conversely, that intense involvement in polity or economy depresses the birth rate, as witness the fewer children in the higher strata, which are customarily more involved in these realms.

Another way of stating the principle of the limits of action is to say that the number of possible actions increases with the number of actors. However, while im-

74

portant, size of population is not in itself a sufficient index to what a society or a group can or cannot accomplish. For one thing, there are great variations among persons in energy and in capacity to carry out a variety of tasks. An abundance of energy is characteristic of some persons—of great leaders, more often than not— and people in the prime of life have, of course, more energy than old people. In general, one assumes that the greater the physical stamina of the population, the higher is its limit of actions per person.

There is also the fact that the potential of a society always includes its use of commercial energy.[18] The average American uses per year fifty-six times as much nonhuman energy from sources such as petroleum, coal, electricity as the average person in India and four times as much as the average person in the Soviet Union. This 'nonhuman energy' may raise the number of possible actions per person. At present, most nonhuman energy used in society is channeled into the economy and used for production of goods and services (statistics on the amount of energy produced constitute one of the most accurate indicators of the state of an economy). The use of nonhuman sources of energy by the military

[18] A general survey of the effects on society of usage of nonhuman energy is found in Fred Cottrell, *Energy and Society* (New York: McGraw-Hill, 1955). An attempt to state the part played by nonhuman energy in the evolution of culture is found in Leslie A. White, *Science of Culture* (New York: Farrar & Straus, 1949).

has recently expanded beyond the limits of the human imagination. The recent developments of electronic data processing and calculation have led to greater use of nonhuman sources of energy in the administration of men and in the pursuit of knowledge. The social consequences of the use of electronic equipment extend far beyond the displacement of a large, but unknown, number of office workers. The new methods of record keeping and processing enhance an administrator's ability to keep track of his subordinates' actions and to hold them accountable. The consequence in any private or public government seems to be the opportunity for more central planning, the lessening of individual privacy and the exercise of individual discretion. In science, the new electronic methods of calculation will probably give us better means for predicting events affected by a large multitude of factors; for example, ballistic fights, health, weather, and social processes. So far, religion, art and ethics have not made much use of nonhuman sources of energy; it is intriguing to speculate about the forms these realms of society would take should they begin to avail themselves of nonhuman sources of energy to move us toward salvation, beauty, and virtue.

On Mobilization

Only rarely do men actually act at the limit of their capacity. What we call 'mobilization' indicates the ratio of actual to potential actions; it varies from idleness to strenuous effort. We normally live at a modest level of mobilization, and it takes a crisis to give us the realization that we can do a great deal more than we usually do. Every individual has his accustomed level of mobilization, which can be slowly changed by forcing him to engage in a higher or lower number of actions.[19] Thus, in the *long run,* it seems to hold that—

A sustained increase in the number of actions per person leads to a higher accustomed level of mobilization, while a sustained decrease in the number of actions per person leads to a lower accustomed level of mobilization.

If the number of actions in a society increases at a faster pace than its population, the accustomed level of mobilization is squeezed upward. In practice, this happens whenever order, prosperity, knowledge, beauty, sacredness, and virtue increase in a society at a faster pace than its population because order, prosperity, knowledge, beauty, sacredness, and virtue are, in effect, sum totals of different types of actions (*supra,* pp. 67–68). If these clusters of actions grow more slowly than the

[19] This and some of the following ideas about mobilization are taken from William James, *The Energies of Men;* new ed. (New York: Dodd, Mead and Company, 1926).

population, the reverse holds and the accustomed level of mobilization slips. Many developing areas of the world face this situation today: In spite of concerted efforts to the contrary, their populations threaten to expand at a faster rate than their order, prosperity, knowledge and other clusters of actions. The result is low accustomed levels of mobilization, that is, a widespread apathy and idleness.

In the *short run,* it seems to hold that—

> An individual above his accustomed level of mobilization is more apt to lower than to increase his mobilization, but below his accustomed level of mobilization he is more apt to increase it than to lower it.

Thus, above their accustomed level of mobilization, there is a built-in laziness in men, and a built-in exuberance below it. Laziness is counteracted by social reward patterns (see, *infra,* pp. 111–114), and exuberance is counteracted by keeping men busy and channels open for new legitimate activities.

These propositions about mobilization make it easy to understand certain typical patterns of social relations. The general rule is—

> Mobilization above par tends to produce social relations such as those between strangers, mobiliza-

78

tion below par tends to produce social relations such as those between neighbors.

The larger the number of social relations a man maintains, the more he is pushed above his customary level of mobilization. He responds to this by reducing the number of actions in these relations, making his social relations less familiar, less lasting, more sporadic and more specialized (*supra,* pp. 58–59). Furthermore, the more associates he has to keep track of, the higher must be his mobilization. It becomes easier for him if he can respond to them in terms of a few categories, such as occupation, sex, or age. Thus, the larger the number of associations, the stronger the tendency to treat them impersonally (*supra,* p. 60), since this eases the required mobilization.[20] In sum, where the ratio of actions per person increases, mobilization rises and we bring it back to par by treating our associates as strangers, or persons with whom we have less familiar, less lasting, more sporadic, more specialized, and more impersonal relations. Contrariwise, where the ratio is lowered and mobilization is below par, we increase it by treating our associates as neighbors, persons with whom we have more inti-

[20] The effects on social relations that follow from a sheer increase in the number of associates with whom a person must deal are explored in a challenging way in Georg Simmel, *Soziologie: Untersuchungen über die Formen der Vergesellschaftung* (Leipzig: Dunker and Humblot, 1908), ch. 2.

mate, more lasting, less sporadic, less specialized and more personal relations.

In the realm of ideas another regularity can be observed—

A mobilization above par predisposes one to rationalism.

In rationalism (*supra*, pp. 65–66), the most spectacular Western way of coping with the limit of communicative actions, a large number of simple ideas is reduced to a small number of general concepts and themes which enter into fixed relations with each other according to simple rules of reasoning, e.g., the syllogism. In extreme cases, a mobilization above par predisposes one to stereotyped thinking. In the use of stereotypes, the rules of reasoning have been suspended; labels and simplified images take the place of the rich details of the world. Both rationalism and stereotypy seem common among people constantly pushed above their accustomed level of mobilization.

On the Convergence of Ideas

A sociological theory of the convergence of ideas can be expressed in various ways; for example—

A person tends to modify his communications (i.e., descriptions, evaluations, and prescriptions) so that they approximate those found among his associates.[21]

This proposition has many implications. To illustrate, if we call some persons father, mother, aunt, uncle or grandparent, this is clearly not because we have first-hand knowledge of the circumstances of our own conception or that of our relatives, but because other people talk about these persons as such-and-such a relation. Also, if we know nothing of the opinions of a person, but a great deal about the opinions of the persons with whom he associates, we then infer a similarity of his opinions to theirs; if he acquires additional associates, he tends to modify his opinions in the direction of those of his new associates; if he gives up certain associates he also tends to give up opinions peculiar to them. However, for any individual the past is never completely erased, only modified; and the future holds out no promise of a completely new man, only of modification of the existing man. There is, then, a measure of flexibility, and when this measure applies to large numbers of human beings we may observe considerable change in a society over a few years.

[21] In my article, "Compliant Actions" [*Acta Sociologica,* II (1957), pp. 179–210], there is a review of some of the evidence for this proposition as it applies to descriptions and evaluations (*ibid.,* sections 4 and 5).

The theory of convergence does not imply that new ideas spread in a society in a random fashion. Various studies tell us that the acceptance of new ideas takes place in conversations with associates (*supra,* p. 57), and in such conversations one can distinguish a minority of 'influentials' from whom the majority, the 'imitators,' take their cues. The identity of the influentials varies from topic to topic; influentials of ideas about fashion are not necessarily influentials about ideas about politics and television programs, et cetera. In general, it seems to hold that the influentials have more knowledge than their imitators, at least of the topic at hand.[22] It is also reasonable to assume that the influentials are less other-directed (*infra,* p. 90) than the imitators, but no research is available to test this.

More important, the theory of convergence suggests that there will be a strain toward consensus wherever associates representing different markets and organizations meet or wherever markets and organizations share the same members (*supra,* p. 64).[23]

22 *Cf.* Elihu Katz and Paul F. Lazarsfeld, *Personal Influence* (Glencoe, Ill.: The Free Press, 1955).

23 On this and other factors affecting social solidarity, see Emile Durkheim, *De la division du travail social* (Paris: Felix Alcan, 1893). Philip Selznick, in his study *TVA and the Grass-roots* (Berkeley, Calif.: University of California Press, 1949) gives several illustrations of the effects of overlapping memberships and mobility. The T.V.A., in order to utilize and mobilize local groups and agencies for its program, that is, to use the grass-roots approach, invited a large number of local leaders

Increases in outside relations, overlapping memberships, and/or mobility tend to bring an increase in the consensus of communications (i.e., descriptions, evaluations, and prescriptions).

Conversely, organizations and markets or other complex social structures without outside contacts, overlapping memberships, and/or mobility run the risk of develop-

---

of community services and voluntary associations to be part-time members or officials of the Authority (co-option), thus creating overlapping memberships. The non-T.V.A. commitments of these local leaders usually outweighed their involvement in the Authority. They reflected and expressed many local resentments against policies of the Authority, for example, its initial measures of land purchase and conservation. It happened that persons partially salaried by the T.V.A. appeared to testify against it at condemnation hearings, or in other ways took the position of the land-owners against the Authority. Eventually, the T.V.A. had to reverse or modify policies because of pressures from participants with such non-T.V.A. involvements. In terms of mobility, the leadership of the Department of Agricultural Relations of the T.V.A. concentrated in the hands of some four or five men whose professional careers had been in (a) extension services of (b) land grant colleges in (c) the Tennessee area. Their past commitments to these colleges made their decisions as T.V.A. administrators gravitate toward granting such colleges a major share in the project. When new federal agencies such as the Farm Security Administration and Soil Conservation services came into being and competed with the programs of the land grant colleges, these administrators forced the T.V.A. to oppose the new agencies and try to exclude them from the Tennessee Valley. Their past experience with extension work made their methods of solution gravitate toward the grass-root approach used by these services. Their regional Southern background helped them immensely to implement this approach among the white population in the area but it also helped them to neglect to invite a significant participation of the Negro colleges and to neglect typically Negro problems such as farm tenancy.

ing into isolated camps with beliefs, values, and norms incompatible with those of the larger society. Certainly, the teaching and maintenance of uncompromising, unusual or extreme ideas are best accomplished under conditions that restrict outside contacts, overlapping memberships (such as intermarriage), and mobility in and out of the system.

Finally, the theory of convergence suggests that—

> Persons exposed to a wider range of opinions among their associates tend to be less stable in their own opinion.

This presumably accounts for the greater tolerance and somewhat shallower convictions prevalent in great cities, among people engaged in far-flung commerce, among cosmopolitan élites, and, indeed, among those leaders who have more contact with the wide world outside their own group than what is available to the rank and file. By contrast, a certain narrow-mindedness tends to mark those whose course of life never takes them outside their own circle.[24] It should be noted, however, that psychologists have discovered that a rigid and prejudiced narrow-mindedness can appear also among ur-

[24] Many of these ideas are discussed in Georg Simmel, "Die Grosstadte und das Geistesleben," *Jahrbuch der Gehe-Stiftung zu Dresden,* IX (1902–1903), 185–206. See also Pitirim Sorokin and Carle C. Zimmerman, *Principles of Rural-Urban Sociology* (New York: Henry Holt, 1929), ch. 13.

banites who have a low limit of actions and who are anxious and uncertain about their self-evaluation.

A Central Assumption about Motivation

Human motivation is, of course, immensely complex and only good fiction and modern psychotherapy can do justice to all its facets and layers. However, experience in some social sciences has shown that simplified assumptions usually suffice for adequate prediction, not of individual actions, but of the actions of aggregates of persons. Thus, economics has been fairly successful in making predictions on the basis of a single motive, the desire to increase profit. Sociology has, of course, to deal with the entire gamut of motives and can be selective only when specific problems allow simplifications. However, it is reasonable that theoretical sociology pays prime attention only to those motives that affect social events to a more drastic extent. Among them, of course, would be counted several biological needs, such as hunger, thirst, sex, sleep, elimination, to which all social structures make accommodations. Among the huge number of acquired needs, I believe there are some that affect social events much more than others and therefore deserve our attention: Among them is a desire to maintain a comfortable level of mobilization (*supra,* p. 78), a desire for cognitive consonance (*infra,* p. 99), a desire to have fun (*infra,* pp. 117–118), and a desire to maintain favorable evaluations from one's associates.[25] The last desire indicates a motive that can be most effectively manipulated by society, and is, therefore, the most central one in sociological thinking.

We may phrase this central sociological assumption about motivation in this way:

> A person tends to engage in actions that help him maintain the evaluations he receives from his associates at or above a given level considered favorable by him in the given situation.

William James saw the motivational significance of evaluations by associates as early as 1891, when his famous dictum appeared: "A man's social me is the recognition which he gets from his mates. . . . Properly speaking, a man has as many social selves as there are individuals who recognize him and carry an image of him in their mind. To wound any one of these images is to wound him." [26]

[25] There are several different candidates for this list. For example, W. I. Thomas proposed four wishes as having significant effects on social relations: the desire for new experience, the desire for recognition, the desire for mastery, and the desire for security. The satisfaction of these wishes for an individual is granted or denied by associates. It is this circumstance that makes them more interesting to sociologists than any of the numerous listings of needs found in the psychological literature. See William I. Thomas and Florian Znaniecki, *The Polish Peasant In Europe and America,* 2d. edition (New York: Knopf, 1927), p. 73.

[26] William James, *The Principles of Psychology* (New York: Holt, 1891), ch. 10, "The Empirical Self or Me," section 1b.

Concern with favorable evaluations is a broad tent under which we cover such things as preoccupation with approval, recognition, admiration, good will, esteem, love, rank, honor, as well as all the honorific garnishings that come with money, power, competence, holiness. It is abundantly evident in the *hubris,* the excessive pride, that ancient Greek dramatists and their followers (including the contemporary historian Arnold Toynbee) assumed to be the root of all human disaster. And it is equally evident among the forces that lift men to new heights of achievement in economy, polity, science, art, religion, and ethics. In short, a desire for favorable evaluations goeth before a rise as well as a fall.

Only actions that are 'visible,' that is, those that can be accurately described by associates, can be evaluated. Thus, people tend to make visible their favorable attributes, and exaggerations enter social life. And, of course, to avoid unfavorable evaluations, men are apt to keep some actions or attributes hidden from view. In this way, a certain evasiveness seems to enter all social intercourse. However, it follows with equal logic that men concerned with maintaining a given level of evaluation will tend to keep a supremely favorable evaluated action or attribute somewhat under the barrel. In this way, understatements become parts of social intercourse. The fact that variations in visibility have motivational significance is one of the bases for the power of pub-

87

licity. The manipulation of visibility is often a gentle and yet effective device to change people's behavior without issuing new prescriptions or appearing "bossy." [27]

It can be shown that the desire to maintain favorable evaluations from others implies a desire to maintain a favorable self-evaluation. The theory of convergence (*supra,* pp. 80–81) assumes that evaluations such as, "Mr. X is good" will spread among associates, and if the latter include Mr. X himself, he will also evaluate himself as good. Thus a favorable evaluation from others creates a favorable self-evaluation.[28] The desire to maintain favorable self-evaluations has received much illumination in contemporary psychodynamics, in which it is used to explain, among other things, "mechanisms of defense." [29]

---

27 *Cf.* Peter M. Blau, *The Dynamics of Bureaucracy* (Chicago: University of Chicago Press, 1955), pp. 34–44.

28 This is a part of the so-called "theory of the looking-glass self" proposed by Charles H. Cooley in *Human Nature and the Social Order* (New York: Scribner, 1902), pp. 183–185.

29 In our context, psychological defense mechanisms may be viewed as typical ways in which descriptions, evaluations, or prescriptions issued by a person are changed when they threaten the level of favorable evaluation he enjoys. For example, sometimes a man does not admit to anyone, not even himself, that he hates his wife: He keeps insisting that everything is all right in his marriage. He has "repressed" his hostility in order to retain the favorable evaluation he enjoys. Repression is a drastic step; it implies a refusal to acknowledge what is apparent to intimate associates in order to preserve a favorable self-evaluation. Other steps might contribute to the same end. A worker who is doing

Any discussion of the need to maintain favorable evaluations from others must face the difficult problem that all our associates do not have the same relevance for our need to maintain favorable evaluations; it is very important for us to be favorably evaluated by some associates and less important to do well in the eyes of others.[30] Psychoanalysis has stressed the importance we attach to obtaining favorable evaluations from childhood associates, particularly from parents; some contemporary thinkers have stressed that certain persons strive primarily for favorable evaluations from peers, that is, contemporary associates resembling themselves in terms of the positions they occupy. In a well-known discussion

---

a poor job may blame it on his poor equipment. Instead of saying, "I have done a poor job," he says, "The tools were inadequate." Actions that are incompatible with his favorable self-evaluation tend to be described by the actor as acts of other agents: This is the well-known process of "projection." Its typical expression is that "they" are the object of blame, not "me." Another case is the sexually weak man who never misses an opportunity to tell others of his sexual adventures. To protect the evaluation he enjoys, he pictures his actions as being the opposite of what they really are. Actions that are incompatible with his favorable self-evaluation tend to be described by the actor as opposite to or different from what they really are: This is the phenomenon of "reaction-formation." See Anna Freud, *Das Ich und die Abwehrmechanismen* (London: Imago, 1936).

[30] This issue, in my opinion, is the heart of so-called "reference group theory" (see **Robert K.** Merton, *Social Theory and Social Structure*, 2d. ed., Glencoe, Ill.: The Free Press, 1957, chs. 8 and 9), although most of the writings under this heading deal merely with problems of modifications of descriptions, evaluations, and prescriptions, and the problems of compliance to prescriptions.

of the American character, the latter are called 'other-directed.' [31] Another classification of the sources of significant evaluations contrasts associates in neighborly social relations with associates who are relative strangers. Those who seek favorable evaluations from the former have been termed 'local' in their outlook; and those concerned with the evaluations of the latter have been termed 'cosmopolitan' in their outlook.[32]

The two classifications overlap. Thus we have four character types (see chart below) into which individuals

	Associates in the past	Associates in the present	
Associates in relations with neighbors	I "traditional"	II "obliging"	Local
Associates in relations with strangers	III "principled"	IV "flexible"	Cosmopolitan
	Inner-directed	Other-directed	

can be divided on the basis of the source of the evaluation they would like to maintain. Type I, the inner-directed local, is represented by the person who all his life arranges his actions in accordance with ideals inculcated in him by his parents. He strikes the observer as tradi-

[31] David Riesman, *The Lonely Crowd* (New Haven: Yale University Press, 1950).
[32] Merton, *op. cit.*, ch. 10. See also Alvin W. Gouldner, "Cosmopolitans and Locals: Toward an Analysis of Latent Social Roles," *Administrative Science Quarterly*, II (1957–1958), 281–306, 444–480.

tional. Type II, the other-directed local, is represented by the person who shifts his actions in order to be appreciated by whoever happens to be close to him. He strikes the observer as obliging. Type III, the inner-directed cosmopolitan, arranges his actions so as to obtain the approval of ideals he has learned about in the past, for example, in higher education. He strikes the observer as principled. Type IV, the other-directed cosmopolitan, adopts a pattern of action that is approved by whoever is at the moment the distant leader of his organization or that is propagated by the mass media or at the market place. He strikes the observer as flexible. There is no basis, in my opinion, for the assumption that all of contemporary society is becoming other-directed. For one thing, the rapid growth of the medical, legal, teaching and engineering professions in modern society represents, in all likelihood, an increase of people that can be called principled (Type III). However, we do not yet have a satisfactory theory revealing the kind of social structure that produces each type.

On Achievement Motivation

To maintain a favorable evaluation by associates is sometimes complicated by variations in the ways evaluations are gauged. Every evaluative statement has an anchorage point, call this Z, for zero, and a smallest noticeable difference, call this *U,* for unit. In the figure below the evaluation, *E,* is measured by the number of *U*'s from *Z.*

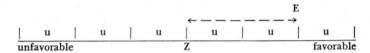

In the statement, "Mr. Smith is a *very good* graduate student," the anchorage point *(Z)* is the average graduate student, the unit of measurement *(U)* is the smallest gradation a professor is able to use when he rates students, and the evaluation *E* ("very good") given to Mr. Smith is one of the higher ones, although not the very highest. It should be clear that an evaluation of Mr. Smith as a graduate student is subject to variations of factors other than Mr. Smith's performance; it will also vary if *Z,* the anchorage point for the judgment, varies perhaps by an influx of very bright students into the class; or if *U,* the unit of gradation, varies through the introduction of a more discriminating examination. Maintaining one's evaluation thus invariably leads to a concern with *Z* and *U.*

People accustomed to receiving high evaluations, e.g., persons who occupy high ranks, thus are particularly likely to defend vigorously the existing scales of ranking and the existing methods of scoring people's standing as high or low. More specifically, we have this theorem—

Persons whose E is above the Z-point of the scale of evaluation tend to resist any movement of the Z-point closer to their E-score, and to resist any inflation in the size of U; while those whose E falls below the Z-point tend to resist any movement of the Z away from their E-score, and to resist any deflation in the size of U.

However, changes in the scoring system often are beyond control. If the Z-point moves closer to a person's E-score and/or if the U's separating them become inflated, then the person has to increase his E-score in order to maintain the same evaluation.[33] Like Alice in Wonderland, he has to run faster to keep in the same place. To maintain his standing, he has to embark on efforts to achieve ever higher evaluations. He is no longer a 'consolidator' of the evaluations he receives, but an 'achiever' of higher evaluations.[34]

The components Z and U are descriptions shared by persons, and therefore subject to influence from associates, according to the law of convergence (*supra,* p.

[33] A very readable use of this argument in the field of economic consumption is found in Thorstein Veblen, *The Theory of the Leisure Class* (New York: Macmillan, 1899), chs. 2–4.

[34] Pareto's discussion of the activities of "lions" and "foxes" in politics and of "speculators" and "rentiers" in the economy contributes much to the understanding of consolidators and achievers, although his terms are defined differently. See Vilfredo Pareto, *Trattato di sociologia generale* (Florence: G. Barbera, 1916), esp. paragraphs 2231–2235.

81). A person remains a consolidator so long as his life-cycle brings him into contact with persons who share his conceptions of Z and U. However, should he by some circumstance, e.g., when engaged in an outside relation, or when his memberships overlap, or in a process of mobility between positions, encounter a higher Z-point or inflated U's, he becomes an achiever, "keeping up with the Joneses." Achievers, therefore, are born mostly in these social structures when such encounters are frequent, for example, in urban settings and in periods of rapid change. It is worth noting that prevalence of achievement motivation and of social consensus (*supra,* p. 83) thus have a determinant in common, and are not as disparate as is usually assumed.

Consolidators and achievers differ somewhat in the kind of social influence they are prepared to accept from associates (according to the theory of convergence, *supra,* p. 81). Generally, it holds that a person's tendency to adopt as his own the ideas of his associates increases to the extent he receives favorable evaluations from his associates. However, the achiever not only adopts ideas from past or present associates but also those of his anticipated future associates. Since such associates hopefully will be in a higher strata, the achiever's opinions tend to be like those of his superiors.

The Knowledge of Social Theorists

On Compliance with and Deviance from Prescriptions

The desire to maintain favorable evaluations by our associates is the key to our compliance with prescriptions. Some central ideas about compliance and deviation are expressed in this twofold proposition:

> The more a person visibly deviates from a prescription given by his associates, the more unfavorable evaluations the latter tend to give him; and this tendency to evaluate him unfavorably is proportionate to the degree to which their own reception of favorable evaluations depends on his compliance with the prescription.[35]

In other words, we enforce our prescriptions by applying sanctions in the form of evaluations to those who violate them, and we are more apt to enforce prescriptions that satisfy us and less apt to enforce those that dissatisfy us.

[35] Several studies supporting the first clause in this proposition have been analyzed by George C. Homans in *The Human Group* (New York: Harcourt Brace, 1950), pp. 140–144, 179–181; and by Henry W. Riecken and George C. Homans in the first part of their chapter, "Psychological Aspects of Social Structure," in *Handbook of Social Psychology*, ed. by G. Lindzey (Cambridge, Mass.: Addison-Wesley, 1954), pp. 786–832, esp. pp. 788–791. The second clause is added here. It is illustrated by an experiment by Stanley Schachter, "Deviation, Rejection and Communication," *Journal of Abnormal and Social Psychology*, XLVI (1951), 190–207.

The proposition makes clear that the motivation to obey prescriptions is always present, since those who deviate are given the unfavorable evaluation which our central motivational assumption asserts that they tend to avoid. Again it is interesting to note that persons who have an achievement motivation will tend to conform, not merely to the prescriptions of their past and present associates, but will adopt actions in the present that may be approved by future mates. Several such instances of anticipatory compliance have been recorded in the literature.

Prescriptions are, of course, violated at times, but only under certain conditions already implied. First, if a prescription is not known to a person, there is no reason to expect that he will obey it. Stupidity, as well as isolation from sources of knowledge about what is expected, breeds deviation. Second, if the action prescribed is not visible to associates, sanctions obviously cannot be forthcoming. Thus, darkness and privacy also breed deviations. Third, if the deviating action is not attributable by the associates to anyone in particular, then sanctions will not be applied to the actor; hence, the less identifiable the actor, the greater the likelihood of violation. The marked deviations that occur in milling, anonymous crowds find their explanation here. Fourth, if a greater reward can be obtained from violating a prescription than from obeying it, the chance of violation increases. There is always a strong temptation to violate a prescription if the violater thereby obtains a higher rank or the prestige associated with a greater command of an institutional value (*infra*, p. 111). Also, if a person is subject to contradictory prescriptions ('role conflict'), he is likely to disobey the one that leads to the lesser reward. Finally, and perhaps most interesting, violations occur when the would-be enforcers withhold sanctions because they gain nothing by applying them. Thus, those who are themselves frustrated by the prescription make poor enforcers. In any group with frustrating prescriptions, enforcement from outsiders becomes essential: It is impossible for the group to "police themselves" effectively.

It is customary to regard deviations as a social evil. However, a certain number of small pockets of deviant behavior and thought may be a useful resource in adapting to drastically changing conditions. If an organization, institutional realm or society is faced with novel and threatening conditions that cannot be handled by the customary means, it is highly useful to have a repertoire of deviant approaches available which can be tried. Thus, those who advocate federal control over what is now state's rights may be unconstitutional deviants today, but may be the only ones who have a workable solution when a national emergency requires concerted national action. Or, those who want to dispense with practically all federal control are deviants today but have a most workable scheme if a natural or military catastrophe hits Washington. Likewise, those who advocate and plan for a preventive war may be deviants today but our saviors in a different turn of history. Or, those who are pacifists may be deviant dreamers today, but in a future situation in which nuclear destructive energy is getting completely out of hand they may have the only key to survival. The urban society with its high level of tolerance of deviation (*supra,* p. 84) stands actually a better chance of survival than the simple, sturdy rural society. And, a democratic society with its prescribed tolerance of deviant ideas has actually greater flexibility in meeting new conditions than the seemingly strong dictatorship which ruthlessly suppresses all deviance from the officially approved pattern.

On the Emergence of Ideas

The following hypothesis is offered—

> New communicative actions (descriptions, evaluations, prescriptions) emerge among associates to the extent that their mobilization is below par, and these new actions become shared and lasting to the extent that they satisfy some recurrent and commonly felt need.

98

Among persons mobilized below par, there is an exuberance manifested as a series of more or less random activities, including communications (*cf. supra,* p. 78). One of these may, by chance, satisfy a need and thus, according to a well-known law of learning, it becomes repeated. Associates take notice of such a repeated communication (a well-known law of perception), and it then follows from the theory of convergence (*supra,* p. 81), that they begin to express it among themselves. If they also are mobilized below par, any such activity is welcome; but, more important, if the new communication contributes to the satisfaction of their recurrent needs, they will continue to embrace it. Thus, a spiraling or growing series of "feelers" are tendered somewhat as in a process of flirtation or seduction until the new idea is accepted.[36]

A difficulty in this reasoning is posed by the lack of an accepted way of identifying man's needs. Promising attempts have been made to use simplified assumptions about needs. For example, if we postulate a need in the individual to reduce cognitive dissonance we arrive at a general principle: Persons tend to embrace new opinions and engage in new actions that are consonant with their past communications and actions.[37]

New descriptions of the social or natural world

---

[36] Albert Cohen, "A General Theory of Subcultures," in his *Delinquent Boys* (Glencoe, Ill.: The Free Press, 1955), ch. 3.
[37] Festinger, *op. cit.*

emerge as a result of information-seeking activities relevant to the satisfaction of felt needs. Information is sought if it reduces cognitive dissonance and is avoided if it adds to dissonance. At times information-seeking activities also appear related to a seemingly universal need to avoid unpleasant surprises, at other times to an apparently equal universal need to avoid the boredom of mobilization below par. In all, however, not much is known about the emergence of new descriptions. More specific statements can be made, however, about the emergence of prescriptions.

A universal fact is the emergence of prescriptions to obtain some measure of insurance against interruption while satisfying nourishment, toilet, sleep, and sex needs, e.g., in the form of norms prescribing respect for privacy. Equally common seem prescriptions that uphold a reasonably even level of mobilization of effort: Excessive idleness becomes prohibited and overdemanding assignments are ruled out. A need to maintain favorable evaluations can be assumed as operative behind a variety of prescriptions. Good examples are provided by the pressures toward tenure found everywhere. For better or worse, we ought to stay married; win or lose, the employer should not arbitrarily discharge employees; competent or senile, the professor still has the right to his chair; gerrymandering or fraud, incumbents insure their re-election. Any competition in the markets of brides, jobs, or goods, ideas, power, etc., implies the risk of losing and being degraded. Therefore, the pressure is always there to replace the competition with "sure deals," and prescriptions emerge in favor of ascriptive positions and less contingent social relations (*supra*, p. 56 and p. 58).

Evaluations of groups can be further guaranteed through other means. Thus, secrecy prescriptions arise to prevent outsiders from obtaining information that lowers the esteem in which a group is held or gives opponents an advantage; discriminatory norms in a group assure that familiar associations with low-ranking persons will not degrade the group. Also, some protection against the shame of devaluation is obtained through eligibility rules. Thus, prescriptions tend to emerge which prohibit persons or groups from entering into pursuits which are beyond their abilities and resources.

The task of protecting individuals from the vagrancies of markets usually falls upon the leaders of their groups. Many leadership decisions are, therefore, prescriptions designed to maintain the accustomed social relations within an organization from becoming too disrupted by events on the outside. Thus, parents attempt to protect their children from the competitions and struggles which they are not yet strong enough to handle; industry executives attempt to soften the impact of market changes on production routines; union leaders

101

Social Theory and Social Practice

try to protect their men from the raw impact of the forces of the labor market; and national leaders try to steer the ship of state so that the big events of international politics do not overly disturb domestic patterns. As people come to rely on these protective mediators to the outside world they tend to idealize and even worship them.[38] The same holds for any social arrangement believed to accomplish the same purpose, such as independence from colonial rule, union shop and freedom from state interference in business. In short, anything perceived to maintain the social order from disruption by outsiders or outside events is given a highly emotive evaluation. This is actually a special case of a more general proposition about the emergence of emotive evaluations that has been used in several scholarly attempts to come to terms with the origin and development of religion in society—

> Anything perceived as maintaining the favorable evaluations received by individuals becomes subject to their emotive evaluation.

Thus, loyalty, idealization, and worship falls upon those men and those social devices that are believed to maintain the social order immune from changes imposed by forces beyond control. We may note in passing that un-

[38] Cf. the discussion of "charisma" by Max Weber, op. cit. pp. 753–757.

der democracy such men are likely to be elected to office. Here lies an explanation of the serious dilemma of democratic nations: In a time when most democracies need to act concertedly to survive and need capital, knowledge, military aid, health services, and consumer goods from each other, each nation is apt to elect rulers who denounce foreign influence and who insulate their states in independence and neutrality.

Some Laws about Markets

Men engaged in advertising and marketing concern themselves with the market responses to offerings announced by various calls (*supra,* p. 63). The general problem faced here, however, is broader than so-called "market research": Theoretical principles need to be formulated which predict such phenomena as what political moves will be accepted by the electorate, what scientific ideas will gain widespread acclaim in a discipline, what technical innovations will be generally adopted, et cetera. In short, we need propositions about the diffusion of market responses.

The first and simplest law here is that—

> The larger the population reached by the market call of any offering, the greater is the popular response.

103

For example, the greater the number of people who receive an advertisement through the mail, the greater the number who will respond to its message; increased mailings never decrease the popular response. The only factor that saves our mailboxes from completely bulging over with mail advertisements is the diminishing financial return to the mailer which forces him to limit his mailings to proven lists of customers presumed to have a greater return rate. The relation between the spread of the market call and the size of the response becomes perhaps less trivial when we deal with highly special, devious, or sophisticated offerings: Somewhat paradoxically, the principle then implies that they cannot succeed unless they are directed to very large populations. A call to establish an association for madrigal music has little chance to succeed when directed to a village or small town. But when addressed to a big city or metropolis there is much better chance to find a sufficient number of interested persons. The big population centers, therefore, tend to contain pockets of specialized and unusual market responses. Some of these are likely to be avant garde, unorthodox, and even criminal. This is one reason why big city life is the most fertile growing ground for new culture (*cf. supra,* p. 84 and p. 94).

A variation of the above line of thought may also be mentioned as our second law of market response—

> The greater the variety of offerings in a market call, the greater the response.

A department store draws more customers than a specialty shop. The requirement to cater to every conceivable interest in the market place is particularly strongly felt by those who want to have a large popular following, be it a church, a retail store, a radio network, or a political party.

A third law of market response is equally simple, yet very useful for predictive purposes—

> The greater the number of opportunities available to a population to heed a market call, the greater is its market response.

For example, the number of persons who will respond to a campaign to visit national parks varies directly with the number of parks within reach. To grow up within reasonable distance of a high school or a college greatly increases the response from the call for higher education; this factor may be as powerful an influence on enrollment as the factor of economic means in the student's family. Likewise, voting increases with the number of polling places, gambling increases with the number of gambling outlets, book reading increases with the number of book stores and libraries, and thefts increase with the number of unlocked premises. Again we can take note of the rich opportunities offered by large cities, and hence the superior market responses obtained here.

In any market, there is a predictable relation between the availability of an offering, the need for it, and the degree to which it is favorably evaluated—

> If the need is constant, an increase in availability of an offering lowers the evaluation of it, and if availability is constant, an increase in the need for it brings a more favorable evaluation to it.

This familiar supply-demand formulation from economics seems to apply also to attitudes and ranks. The popularity of a hit tune or a new fashion, a new TV or radio program, a new style of architecture or art, increases so long as new people learn about and demand it, but it decreases with the number of copied or plagiarized versions that become available. Likewise, occupational skills in demand at any particular time may be a factor in advancing the prestige of an occupation while, conversely, abundantly available skills command little occupational prestige. The same seems to hold for personal prestige: Popular admiration is rarely accorded the typical citizen; it is given to the extraordinary citizen, one who has an unusual background or superior vision and adeptness in his field. (Contrary to much that is said on this point, I maintain that democracies, which select leaders by a kind of general-attitude census, are not likely to elect either mediocre or so-called common men to high office.)

On Evaluative Equalization

It is normal in our type of society for an individual to have commitments to more than one organization or market at the same time. Thus, during the course of an ordinary day or week a person may have to act at times in his occupational role, at times as a family man, at times as a bridge partner, at times as a church member, and so on. His respective ranks in these various positions are not, necessarily, all on the same level. Whenever a person with a constellation of ranks appears in a high-ranking capacity, his evaluation is favorable, but whenever he has to appear in his low-ranking capacity his relative evaluation declines. This kind of riding on the social roller coaster is inconsistent with our assumption about motivation to maintain a favorable evaluation (*supra,* p. 86). Thus—

> If a person is evaluated much less favorably in one activity than in others, he will tend either to withdraw from that activity or to attempt to raise the

evaluation received in that activity to a level commensurate with evaluations received in the others.

Persons who engage in respected occupations tend to belong to high-prestige churches; to join prestigious organizations; to participate in exclusive recreational activity and to marry into families of good lineage (*cf. infra,* p. 115). This entire process may be solidified by prescriptions. The degradation regularly experienced by persons who hold discrepant ranks sets in motion the process of emerging norms (*supra,* pp. 98–101) and new prescriptions emerge which restrict or prohibit rank discrepancies. For example, if a daughter marries below her family's station, the in-law position of the members of the family will rank lower than their other positions. This decrease in favored evaluations will start the process of emergence, and the prescription, "Don't marry that man" appears.

On Familiarity in Social Relations

If we take a statistical view of success and failure (i.e., assuming that some failures are inevitable), it follows that—

> The larger the number of actions, relations, and positions entering our composite evaluation of an

actor, the less likely it is that this evaluation will fluctuate.

This proposition makes it possible for us to identify some situations in which the nature of the social relations affects the maintenance of favorable evaluations.

First, less familiar relations (*supra,* p. 59) expose the participants to greater risks of being devaluated than more intimate ones. The greater the number of a person's actions that are known about and evaluated by others, the smaller the risk of his being unfavorably evaluated for any single or occasional failure or slip. Second, the smaller the number of relations that a person enters into, the greater his risk of being downgraded. A person in only one social relation is putting all his eggs in one basket, gambling on success in this role. If, on the other hand, an individual invests the same number of actions in several social relations, it is likely that a failure in one will be balanced by success in others, and on the whole, he stands a better chance of maintaining a favorable evaluation from others. In short, having additional social relations, preferably of an intimate kind, serves to maintain a person's favorable evaluation when he embarks on pursuits exposing him to fluctuating evaluations.

The first researchers in industrial sociology were surprised to find great familiarity and informality superimposed on the formal job organization. The urbanization and industrialization of Western Europe brought about an upsurge in friendly voluntary association in the nineteenth century. Similarly, contemporary so-called underdeveloped countries seem to emerge with the same rich flora of associations when their social structure changes toward that of a modern society. And long before, De Tocqueville, observing the settlers from aristocratic Europe in achievement-stressing America, was surprised by the abundance of voluntary associations they created in their new land. In all these instances, we might assume that the new associations help to maintain a certain inner security among the participants in the face of threats to their new status. It should be realized, however, that the hypothesis merely states that a certain aggregate of persons will have a motive to form or enter in some secure or risk-spreading social relations. Whether or not they will actually do so is a different issue, one that depends on the opportunities opened to them by their position in the social structure. If they are aready involved in some social relation characterized by familiarity and informality they may revitalize and intensify their participation in them. If they have access to already existing groups that meet these criteria they may join them. If they do not know any such groups but interact with others who have the same motive, such a group may be formed.

110

On Institutional Reward Patterns

We recall that science, polity, economy, religion, art, and ethics are the institutional realms of society. Each one of these realms has an institutional value: Thus, knowledge, prosperity, order, beauty, sacredness and virtue are the institutional values corresponding to these realms. Also, each of these institutional realms has its typical mode of stratification: We said that command of knowledge defines competence, control of social order defines power, command of prosperity defines riches; likewise, command of beauty indicates taste, command of the sacred indicates holiness, and command of virtue indicates moral "rectitude" (*supra,* pp. 67–70).

The desire to maintain favorable evaluations from others (*supra,* p. 86) is also one key to people's concern with their institutional values.

> The more visible control of an institutional value (prosperity, knowledge, etc.) a person has, the more favorable evaluations he receives from his associates.

Thus men of competence, power, riches, taste, sacredness and rectitude are more likely to receive favorable evaluations than others. Perhaps it is even likely that

111

women are more apt to fall in love with such men than with others.

Each institutional realm has potentially a typical 'institutional reward pattern' which provides for a regular relation between a degree of control over an institutional value and the receipt of specified honorific rewards. Such patterns, in which changes in control of institutional values are automatically related to changes in specified honorific rewards, are a strategic object of sociological study.[39]

In the Western economy, the signs of success honored by the larger community consist of visible goods and services, number of residences (rated as to size and location), number of employees and labor-saving devices, annual charity and (in some countries) taxation contributions, and, in the case of firms, annual reports of earnings. Often the economic reward pattern also allows the successful individual to attach his name to his enterprise (e.g., the Ford Motor Company, the Krupp Works). In many instances there is a certain automatism —success by virtue of success—in economic rewards. For example, the successful individual may become a creditor and investor, receiving additional income in the form of interest or dividends—and homage from those

---

[39] The only one that so far has been subject to systematic analysis is the reward pattern of science. See Robert K. Merton, "Priorities in Scientific Discovery: A Chapter in the Sociology of Science," *American Sociological Review*, XXII (1957), 635–659.

who may want to borrow money from him. Note that the reward pattern is further solidified by a series of prescriptions; for example, if a rich man does not show a normal amount of display of wealth he may be denounced as a miser, and if a visitor to the successful does not choose to notice or appreciate displayed goods and services, he may be denounced as ungrateful or snobbish.

In the contemporary polity, the reward pattern centers on symbols of position, such as titles and uniforms, on constant publicity and evaluation by mass media, on approval from cheering masses, on ceremonial rights and decorations. Successful men may also have cities, roads, bridges, public buildings, acts of legislation, and the like named in their honor; they may have statues, portraits, and memorial plaques created to commemorate their deeds. An ultimate evaluation, here as in other fields, may be the judgment of future historians.

In science, a firmly established pattern ties the name of the scientist to his published contributions to knowledge. Scientific articles and monographs get into print only if they contain new knowledge, and a scientist's own publications are often more dear to him than his worldly possessions. And any new scientific report is expected to recognize in text or footnotes the authors of the more relevant ideas entering as parts of a new discovery, technique, or argument.

In religion, various signs make visible how close a

113

person is to the sacred (for example, special gifts of tongue or admissions to a graded series of holy rites) and call forth reverence by the community. The ultimate basis of the religious reward pattern is, of course, the evaluation of people by the divine assumed by believers. The typical service in Christian churches goes through a regular sequence in which an emphasis on the fact that man's evaluation is lowered because of the sins he has committed is followed by an emphasis on God's restoration of this evaluation through the forgiveness of sins.

In art, the reward pattern is less clear-cut. For a contemporary painter, for example, it would include the number of his private shows, the number and kind of reviews by critics, the rating of the galleries in which his paintings have been exhibited, the number and prominence of the collectors who have acquired his paintings, the number of his paintings hanging in museums.

In ethics, Western culture has not developed any elaborate reward pattern, and the badges of moral rectitude are few; while virtue is, of course, appreciated, to do it visible honor is widely thought to cancel it out. Only history can tell whether this lack in Western culture will prove significant or not.

Given the relation expressed in the proposition that if an institutional value is growing, the evaluation given to those who control shares of it becomes more favorable, it follows that whatever is a typical evaluation is subject to constant revision upward. In other words, when an institutional value grows, the Z-point in the corresponding reward pattern is moving upward. However, as was argued (*supra*, p. 94), this upward movement is a circumstance in which an achievement motivation is generated. Thus—

> When institutional values are expanding, achievers appear.

This is indeed convenient: Where expansions have created new opportunities, achievers emerge to take advantage of them.

Another implication may also be noted. If the principle relating control of institutional values to receipt of favorable evaluations is combined with the principle of evaluative equalization an important deduction emerges. Those who experience a rise in their control of one institutional value are likely to feel a certain pressure to acquire control of other institutional values as well. Thus it happens that—

> The modes of stratification in various institutional realms tend to cluster.[40]

[40] *Cf.* Emile Benoit-Smullyan, "Status, Status Types, and Status Interrelations," *American Sociological Review*, IX (1944), 151–161.

Those who rank high in terms of one want to become high in others as well.

On Differentiation of Positions and Communications between Ranks

It is still somewhat of a mystery how division of labor emerges in a society. However, one simple principle may be mentioned—

> Among associates, the positions of those performing different actions (or very dissimilar distributions of the same actions) are likely to become differentiated.

Careful studies have shown how kinship positions, such as mother and aunt, brother and male cousin, become differentiated. Thus we know that the presence of factors equalizing some kinsmen's actions (e.g., common sex, generation, residence, and descent) make it likely that the same kinship term (i.e., position) will be assigned to these kinsmen, while conversely, the presence of factors differentiating actions of relatives leads to a severality of kinship positions among them.[41]

The differentiation of positions according to institutional realms, economic, political, religious, and so on,

41 George P. Murdock, *Social Structure* (New York: Macmillan, 1949), esp. ch. 7.

is a more complex issue. Since each institutional realm has its characteristic action type (*supra,* p. 67), the principle of differentiation of positions is relevant here too. In practice, however, I would guess that the development of some distinct institutional reward patterns is needed to differentiate an institutional realm as a more separate unity.

Within institutional realms positions tend to assume varying ranks. This makes for much of the drama of social intercourse. We may meet our associates either as superiors in rank, equals, or inferiors in rank. The rewards in these social relations differ. The good superior receives 'deference' and the good inferior receives 'care.' Both deference and care have a favorable self-evaluation as a common denominator. But the true equal has 'fun,' the delight and joy of being together in play. Only equals meet in 'play.' When inferiors and superiors meet there is always 'work' of one kind or another. The desire to have fun is a motive that deserves more than passing attention.[42] Because fun is available only in equalitarian relations, however temporary they may be, it is an antidote to rank and to concern over favorable evaluations from others. From time to time most superiors give up the deference of their high position to enjoy the fun and joy of play with equals, and if left

---

[42] *Cf.* Erving Goffman, *Encounters* (Indianapolis, Ind., Bobbs-Merrill, 1961), pp. 15–81.

alone, inferiors are likely to turn work into play to share its joy. However, the fun of play is not forever; it disappears as soon as someone fails to act as an equal or as soon as someone through a tactless remark makes the participants aware of their differences in riches, power, education or taste.

It appears that the presence of an institutional realm that lacks clear-cut stratification facilitates interaction between people with positions in more stratified institutional realms. For instance, a religion that does not allow much of the "holier than thou" sentiment may serve as a meeting ground where people of different ranks in economy, polity, and science can get together in some sense of equality. Such a religion serves as an integrative force in society.[43] It combines the joy of equalitarian relations with the social cement of overlapping memberships and outside contacts (*supra,* pp. 82–83).

On Vested Interests and on Class Conflicts

Each institutional value, we recall, has creators, purveyors, and receivers. Knowledge is developed by scholars, transmitted by teachers, and received by students; persons who produce modifications in the social order

---

43 *Cf.* Emile Durkheim, *Les forms élémentaire de la vie religieuse* (Paris: Alcan, 1912).

are rulers, those who apply or transmit their prescriptions are administrators, and those who are at the receiving end are the subjects (*supra,* p. 68). The reward patterns linking institutional values to favorable evaluations vary a great deal in different historical circumstances (*supra,* pp. 112–114). We can now further specify that—

> Institutional reward patterns are differently elaborated by, respectively, the creators, purveyors, and receivers of an institutional value.

Persons sharing a common style of life centered on their particular reward pattern form a 'vested interest.' The distinctions we made between creators, purveyors and receivers of various institutional values are likely to reappear as distinctions between vested interest groups. Their concern with the elaboration and protection of their reward patterns generates much of the dynamics in a society. The great sociologist, Max Weber, focused much of his attention on vested interests, and his writings lend support to the assumption that much of human history is a contest between various vested interest groups.[44]

[44] Weber's historical writings contain analyses of patrimonial vassals, Junkers, officers, civil servants, priesthoods, and several other vested interests. The German term used by Weber for these vested interests is "Stand." It is formally defined in Max Weber, *op. cit.,* p. 179, and sometimes rendered in English as "status group."

119

This assumption tends to correct somewhat the one-sidedness in the Marxian dictum that all history is a struggle between classes. The class struggles are cases in which organized aggregates of those who control a small share of an institutional value—especially prosperity and order—revolt against those who control a large share.[45] Since there is a positive relationship between control of an institutional value and the evaluations received from others, it follows that the people in the lower strata have to accept a lower estimate of their worth. Herein lies the motivational basis for class struggles; the lower strata take over the methods of measuring worth that prevail in the higher strata. One may say that a 'class' line or a class cleavage is experienced wherever or whenever a relatively low stratum measures its worth according to criteria prevalent in a relatively high stratum. The closer a person is to the upper strata, the more likely he is to adopt their Z's and U's (*supra*, p. 93). In other words, the feeling of degradation arises earliest and becomes strongest in the upper segments of the lower strata, from where it may, through agitation, spread

45 For a useful compilation of the most important of the references to class and class conflicts scattered through the writings of Karl Marx, see Tom B. Bottomore and Maximilian Rubel, eds., *Karl Marx: Selected Writings in Sociology and Social Philosophy* (London: Watts, 1956), pp. 178–202. A critical but sympathetic modern review applying Marxian ideas to "industrial" (rather than "capitalist") societies is found in Ralph Dahrendorf, *Class and Class Conflict in Industrial Society* (Stanford, Calif.: Stanford University Press, 1959).

120

downward. We talk about a class struggle when these sentiments permeate militant organizations and are not merely individual reactions. The legitimacy of the existing mode of stratification is denied by these class organizations and a new scoring of social worth is proposed, in which the last shall become the first and the first the last. The Marxists typify this ethos in the *Internationale:*

> No more tradition's chains shall bind us
> Arise, you slaves; no more the thrall!
> The earth shall rise on new foundations,
> We have been naught, we shall be all!

In spite of the appeal of such protest ideologies, history shows no exception to the rule that class struggles succeed only in modifying existing stratification or in replacing one form of division by another. In no society, ever, has stratification been abolished or equal control of institutional values been achieved by all.

There are several devices, planned or unplanned, that channel the resentment generated by the frustrations of the members of the lower strata away from a frontal attack on their superiors on the other side of the class line. The simplest is allowing the more intelligent among the frustrated to rise into higher strata. Upward social mobility reduces the potential for class conflict. To have a father, brother or son on the other side of a class line balances class loyalty against family loyalty; as usual, mobility and overlapping memberships keep groups together, rather than apart (*supra,* p. 83). The frustrated group may also be diverted from economic and political realities and interested in other types of comparison. This refocusing may be in terms of the stratification in other realms of society, as in the case of a religious faith that grants a place in heaven regardless of a person's economic or political standing. The modern world also has other features that provide alternative rankings. One is concern with sports and athletics. The critical comparisons of men of money, power, and competence made by, say, mass media are never as sharp as the comparisons of athletes or ball players. Another distraction is concern with celebrity. The mass media not only draw attention to men of power, class, competence; they also focus on café society, thus helping their public to confuse high positions in the stratification system with ability to get in the way of camera lenses. Finally, gambling provides the stuff out of which dreams of a spectacular improvement in station are made through no major effort of one's own. Innocent fantasies obviate both upward mobility and class-conflict. Gambling activities are more prevalent in segments of society right below a class line than in other segments of society.

The Knowledge of Social Theorists

On Humanitarianism

It is an old observation that persons who suffer give favorable evaluations to those who relieve their sufferings. Appreciation is given those who help the weak, care for the sick, console the sorrowing, regardless of whether there are prescriptions to be helpful. Thus, a 'humanitarian' motivation is possible wherever sufferings occur—and that, of course, is virtually everywhere. Since violence always results in suffering, humanitarianism grows with the use of violence; it is perhaps not accidental that the Red Cross is a product of war. At times entire organizations and markets become involved in such humanitarian enterprises and a "welfare establishment" emerges with its own reward patterns. In fact, in modern so-called welfare states, the welfare establishment has many of the characteristics of a full-fledged institutional realm.

Persons whose favorable evaluations are maintained through a larger than usual share of humanitarian acts are called 'tender-hearted.' In contrast, those who strive for their evaluations in other endeavors than humanitarian ones—for example, the pursuit of money, power, or academic excellence—are called 'tough-minded.' This is a useful distinction in many situations, above all, perhaps, in characterizing leaders. In general, I should say that organization men tend to become tender, while market men tend to be tough. By being tender-hearted, the organization man receives support that he needs from his fellow members; by being tough-minded, the market man loses support he needs less from competitors and adversaries. Traditionally, women have remained within the organization of the household and have developed a reputation for being the tender sex, while men have entered the market places of work and politics, establishing the image of being the tougher sex.

On Oscillation of Dominant Motivational Types

A useful typology emerges when humanitarianism is cross-classified with achievement motivation. Tough-minded achievers may be called 'pioneers,' and tender-hearted achievers 'reformers.' Tough-minded consolidators I shall call 'protectors' and tender-hearted ones 'philanthropists' (see chart).

	Achievers	*Consolidators*
Tough-minded	Pioneers	Protectors
Tender-hearted	Reformers	Philanthropists

One might argue that there is a certain pattern of oscillation throughout the history of a society (or an institutional realm) between these types. Phases in

124

which tough-minded people dominate seem to be followed by phases in which tender-hearted people dominate; and phases in which achievers dominate seem to be followed by phases in which consolidators dominate. However, this idea needs much further development to be useful in diagnosing historical trends.[46] A possible cyclical pattern is this: When pioneers, that is, tough-minded achievers, dominate for a time, they generate much suffering, consequently more tender-hearted achievers emerge. This, however, takes some of the steam out of the institutional growth (*infra,* p. 127), so that achievement motivation becomes less prevalent; thus, more consolidators emerge in the form of both tough-minded protectors and tender-hearted philanthropists. Then philanthropists get into contact with the underprivileged, giving bonanzas and encouragement, and thus generate new achievement motivation (*supra,* p. 94), and a new generation of pioneers or reformers is born, starting the cycle all over again.

On Growth of an Institutional Value

Little is known about the causes of expansion, even though there is a great deal of concern all over the world today about the ways in which a nation grows in prosperity, order, knowledge, virtue. In contemplating any

46 *Cf.* Vilfredo Pareto, *The Rise and Fall of Elites* (New York: The Bedminster Press, 1962).

large collection of case histories of institutional development one cannot avoid the conclusion that the development never proceeds evenly. Phrases such as "boom and
bust" and "rise, realization, exhaustion and decline"
come to mind. Small fluctuations in growth and decline
are understandable in principle. Growth of an institutional value, by definition, is an expansion in the prevalence of a certain type of action (*supra,* p. 67). As
has been said (*supra,* p. 106), any change in availability
of an action changes the evaluation of it (if demand is
constant). Thus, the creators of an institutional value
are apt to overproduce it when evaluations are high and
underproduce it when evaluations are low, and these
changes in the supply of the institutional value generate
fluctuations in evaluations that lead to a new cycle of
overproduction and underproduction.

These fluctuations provide great challenges for achievers (*supra,* p. 93). The most daring among them attempt
to rise with the tide when the trend is upward and to
enjoy tenure in one form or another when the trend is
downward. Thus, the ambitious scientist may capitalize
on a specialty in his field in which knowledge is rapidly
expanding. When worth-while discoveries in this area
become less likely, he withdraws to rest on his laurels
(e.g., in the form of a university chair), or switches to
another specialty in expansion. Likewise, the ambitious
investor and politician throw their lot wherever oppor-

tunities expand and stay on the sidelines with their nest egg of capital and good will when opportunities decline. Of course, all ambitious achievers, particularly the less intelligent, run the risk of misjudging the trends and thus being stuck with whatever they have when others advance, or lose what they have when others enjoy their share in relative security. In all, however, it is fair to assume that an institutional value will grow in the hands of intelligent achievers.

Technically speaking, we may tentatively assume a general principle of this kind—

> Growth of an institutional value is a function of the degree to which the institutional value is channeled from its receivers back to its creators.

This return of an institutional value to its creators is what we know as 'investment.' The "multiplier" effect of investment on prosperity is well known in theoretical economics. An original investment generates a chain reaction of progressively smaller investments throughout the economy, and prosperity; the total value of all goods and services increases.

The principle of growth through investment is much more obscure once we leave the economic realm. However, exploring some analogies can be suggestive. When subjects exert pressure (market-call prescriptions in the body politic) on their rulers to regulate some activity, the order grows when they succeed because new prescriptions (laws) come into effect. Moreover, the rulers typically delegate the task of formulating the details of application and enforcement of the prescriptions to trusted officials who, in turn, delegate some task to assistants, and so forth. However, each step of delegation generates new prescriptions which define the authority of the different administrators. Thus, a "multiplier" of sorts operates here; the initial prescription from subjects to rulers adds a generous share of growth to the order in society. In science, the principle of growth through investment suggests that no piece of knowledge must be allowed to rest in idle secrecy. For example, patents must not be bought and suppressed or research findings kept secret: The creators of knowledge will be more successful if every past piece is available to them. In art, the principle suggests that items of beauty should not be scattered about in inaccessible private places but be brought together into magnificent exhibitions or festivals that will inspire the creators of art to new ventures.

Another possibility of growth, also in need of much further study, is that growth in one institutional value may create an opportunity for growth through investment in another value. Thus, an increase in sacredness may provide for new works of art; an increase in knowledge may provide for new profitable products; an increase in prosperity may provide for a new political order. This is one of the most intriguing ways in which events in one institutional realm have consequences in another.

Growth of an institutional value is unsettling in many ways. One of the best documented is this—

> When an institutional value grows, the number of purveyors of the growing institutional value significantly expands.

Thus, when prosperity grows, the ranks of dealers and brokers expand; when the level of knowledge grows, the number of teachers increases; when the social order grows, the number of functionaries and administrators expands. In other words, new middle strata emerge. Far from polarizing the society into two extreme camps of upper and lower classes, as Marx predicted, the most conspicuous feature of societies growing in prosperity is the expansion of the cadres of middlemen, in our times known as "white-collar workers."

BY WAY OF CONCLUSION

Some propositions we have reviewed may be startling. But many others are reformulations of very simple ideas.

Stripped of their technical language, their content is often found to be plain common sense: "A person's thinking and talking is influenced by others he meets"; "Honors come with power"; "Most of the time people do what they are told"; "No one has time or energy to do or see everything"; "People don't like to be stripped of their honors"; "Those who have the same station in life are apt to think alike."

One shortcoming of common sense is that in many instances it fails to combine such simple ideas in a correct way. Let us take an example. Given is the observation that the democratic constitutions and preambles of most voluntary associations are façades behind which oligarchies rule. Very rarely does it happen that chairmen are voted out of office, very rarely is there found organized opposition to parties and platforms. Labor unions are a conspicuous example: Officers continue in office until they retire with pension. There is little debate about polity. All agree on the objective of securing higher wages for union members. The technical discussions as to conditions of employment and other agenda to be negotiated in the talks with management are left to the leaders. Well-informed union men may occasionally feel that their leaders are talking the language of management, but on the whole, they are so loyal to them that only rarely do they show up at annual meetings when the policy is presented and the leaders are re-elected. Common-sense thinking tends to blame this on the personalities involved: The leaders are called "hungry for power"; the membership is called corrupt and "lacking in idealism."

Theoretical sociology, however, can demonstrate that the true explanation of these facts is of a different kind.[47] And the explanation consists precisely of new combinations of the simple ideas suggested above. We know from our assumption about motivation (common-sense version: "People don't like to be stripped of their honors") that actions are arranged so that favorable evaluations of the actors are maintained (*supra,* p. 86). Since leaders, men of power, receive higher evaluations than rank and file members (*supra,* p. 111; common-sense version: "Honors come with power") they are motivated to remain leaders. Simultaneously, the principle of the limits of action (*supra,* p. 74; common-sense version: "No one has time or energy to do or see everything") is in operation, inclining the membership to a more or less apathetic attitude as to what goes on in the association: Work and family life take the larger share of their energy. Since the members receive approximately equal types and amounts of rewards, the theorem

[47] *Cf.* S. M. Lipset's discussion of "Michel's iron law of oligarchy" in "The Political Process in Trade Unons: A Theoretical Statement," in *Freedom and Control in Modern Society,* ed. by Morroe Berger, Theodore Abel, and Charles H. Page (New York: Van Nostrand, 1954), pp. 82–124.

of the emergence of communications predicts that no divergent policies are likely to appear among the members (*supra,* p. 98; common-sense version: "Those who have the same station in life think alike"). In other words, political cleavages inside the union will be at a minimum. All this sets the stage for the perpetuation of a leadership that is to all intents and purposes unchallenged—an oligarchy. The leaders who are thus maintained in office negotiate and interact with leaders of other institutions; in accordance with the convergence theory (*supra,* p. 81; common-sense version: "A person's thinking and talking are influenced by others he meets"), they absorb more and more of what is accepted among their peers in business, politics, and the like. In other words, they become estranged from the values and life of those who elect them and begin accommodating the more privileged groups whom they normally oppose.

Common sense is correct only superficially in attributing this effect to "hunger for power" and "want of idealism": The entire process is predictable from a combination of sociological propositions, each one of which is well known to common sense. The important thing to note is that common sense was unable to make the right *combination* of ideas.

This is fairly typical: Theoretical sociology employs combinations of propositions in systematic ways unlikely to be hit upon by lay thinking. A prime preoccupation of the theoretical sociologist, as I see it, is with the systematic combinations of propositions. His success in this enterprise will determine whether he has anything of value to say to his contemporaries.

The theoretical sociologist is, thus, well advised to be on the lookout for devices that aid him in making correct combinations of simple propositions; among these must be numbered a technical vocabulary—even mathematical and computer language—since ordinary language combines ideas in a rather haphazard manner. If abstract sociological reformulations of common experiences lend themselves to more accurate combinations of ideas than the lay formulations, we must accept them even though they may lack a literary quality. This is not to excuse the terminological excesses that plague sociology, but to indicate that any difficulties with formulations that the reader is likely to have met with in this review of theoretical sociology are, at least in part, inherent in the discipline.

4 The Practical Use of Social Theory Through Scholarly Consultations

In the history of relations between science and the world of affairs there is a relationship of some standing that might be called *the scholarly consultation*. A scientist is asked by a client to look into a problem and tell what ideas for solution are suggested by the knowledge, new or old, in his discipline. The scholarly consultation is a complex event. The following elements, however, seem to be present in any substantive consultation.

Exploratory Inquiry. The consultant finds out the details of the problem. This is usually done simply by talking to the people involved and observing the problem situation at first hand. Sometimes this involves a genuine diagnostic research project, but normally the process is much more informal than a research project.

Scholarly Understanding. The client's problem is translated by the consultant into scientific terms, and the corresponding theoretical problems are formulated. Also, descriptive information of a general kind about the variables entering into the problems are assembled from the consultant's memory, library, or research files.

Scholarly Confrontation. The client is given a perspective on his problem by being told in general language how the scientific discipline views his problem, and he is given a descriptive orientation about some variables entering into his problem.

Discovery of Solutions. The consultant takes the laws of his discipline to calculate the solution (or alternative solutions) to the theoretical problems for which such solutions exist. Thus he obtains what we may call theoretical solutions.

Scientific Advice. The client is presented with a translation of the theoretical solutions into the client's language and with references to his specific situation. In short, he is told what to do. Also, he is given some idea of the complications or unintended consequences that might occur should he adopt the solutions proposed.

I hasten to say that this is not the order in which a consultation proceeds, but these are some of the key elements in the consultation process. In actual practice, the exploratory inquiry goes on almost throughout the entire consultation; the scholarly confrontation may be much needed at the end when the advice is put into perspective, and the discovery of solutions usually goes hand in hand with the formulation of theoretical problems. However, we must be able to distinguish these elements in our discussion because they involve different operations; each has a logic of its own, and a human drama of its own.

Samples from a Consultation

In the winter of 1957–58 a well-known museum in a provincial capital presented this problem:

Over the last few years, the Museum has been very successful in augmenting the size and value of its collection. The Museum has also been successful in extending its facilities and has added a wing with a well-equipped stage where it produces art plays of high quality. In spite of this, the galleries attract few adult visitors, and there are often empty seats at the theatre performances. What can be done to increase the audience response to Museum activities?

There is a good reason for choosing this problem as our illustration. The published literature of sociology contains no studies of museum audiences. Furthermore, the whole field of the sociology of art is very much in its infancy; descriptive facts about public involvement in art are largely missing, and confirmed sociological propositions about art are practically nonexistent. Whatever a sociologist can say about this problem must therefore derive from general sociological knowledge.

Making an Exploratory Inquiry

To discover the details of the problem and examine the setting in which it existed, the consultant visited the Museum for a couple of days, talked to its director and personnel, read the literature that the Museum had published, and participated in its activities. A co-worker spent some afternoons in a library scanning general museum publications, listing typical problems of gallery and theatre administration. On the basis of these explorations, a team of four interviewers was assembled and briefed on the dimensions of the problem as known at that time. This team was brought to the museum town for two days. They interviewed approximately thirty persons who were in a position to know the situation of the arts in the area—art teachers, artists, editors, gallery owners, community leaders, et cetera—and an additional thirty people from all walks of life were simply asked details about their visits to museums, if any. One team member was placed in the Museum gallery to observe visitors during their walk through the museum exhibits, and to talk with them afterward. All

138

members of the team were professional sociologists trained to select comments or events having counterparts in theoretical sociology and to record them in writing. The material collected was not meant to be statistically representative or used in statistical tables. It consisted of a scattering of notes believed to be pieces in the sociological picture puzzle describing the situation of the client and his problem. Much information gleaned this way merely confirmed what the museum director previously had told, but some was novel. All, or practically all, could have been obtained by one consultant working alone; however, the team did it faster than any one man could, and perhaps also helped to make the final description more reliable.

Thus, the exploratory inquiry in this case consisted of a collection of (1) details of how the client describes his problem and general situation and (2) details of how others who are strategically placed view or experience the client's problem and situation. Only those details were assembled by the consultant and his co-workers that could be fitted into the categories of sociology, i.e., phrased in sociological terminology.

No bones should be made about this: The exploratory inquiry never provides complete or impartial descriptions. It is a selective or biased inquiry in which the consultant scans his client's situation, looking primarily for the things that his science pays attention to and knows something about. Each detail is explored only to the point where the consultant feels satisfied that he knows enough of it to fit into his sociological theory. A consultant with different knowledge of theory would explore different details. A brighter and more experienced consultant might be able to find additional events in the client's situation about which theoretical insights are available. A less bright and experienced consultant would record fewer details. Naturally, science also has ways of making more systematic and unbiased descriptions. These are done by researchers, not consultants, according to well-established criteria. Scholarly consultations are, of course, well served by good descriptive research studies, but in their absence an exploratory inquiry is good enough.

Achieving a Scholarly Understanding

The material about the Museum gathered in the exploratory inquiry was put together into a single ringbinder, and read and reread several times with the purpose of establishing the theoretical problems involved. Markers were entered into the binder locating material translatable into theoretical problems and a total of twelve such problems was formulated. We shall review only a few here:

The Response of the Public

What the Museum wants is to increase the response from the public to the various programs and exhibits it offers. Of all our principles of theoretical sociology, the ones dealing with market responses are, therefore, most readily applied to the problem of the Museum. We have discussed three such principles:

A. The larger the population reached by the market call of an offering, the greater is the market response (*supra,* p. 103).
B. The greater the number of opportunities available to a population to heed a market call, the greater is its market response (*supra,* p. 105).
C. The greater the variety of offerings in a market call, the greater the response (*supra,* p. 105).

In our case, the "population" mentioned in (A) is the size of the population reached by the Museum. The "opportunities to heed the market call" mentioned in (B) are people's opportunities to attend Museum programs. Finally, the "variety of offerings" mentioned in (C) is, of course, the varieties of Museum programs. Let us review them in turn.

A. The *size of population* reached and served by the Museum is, in theory, an entire state, but in practice it is the capital of the state, a city of less than 250,000 in-

141

habitants. They are subject to city-wide advertisements about Museum activities in newspapers and through posters. In addition, the Museum advertises its program through direct mail. The amount of advertising done by this Museum appears to be the same or greater than that done by other museums of comparable stature. It seems clear that the Museum has encountered a nation-wide phenomenon that in contemporary America only a handful out of every thousand adults attends art exhibits and plays. In a great metropolis with millions of people, a per cent or two of the population would still number in tens of thousands. Such large cities could easily support several theatres, symphonies, galleries. In a relatively small city of less than 250,000, a per cent or two is only three or four thousand. This fact that the Museum city is relatively small is essential for the understanding of the plight of the Museum.

Observations and interviews make it clear that the response to the Museum offerings is greatest among the economic and political and educational élite in the Museum town. There are many reasons for this—some of which will be reviewed later—but in this context we may simply note that most people who receive direct mail announcements from the Museum belong in these privileged strata.

Below the upper class, interest in the Museum seems to decline progressively. The upper middle class is rather active in Museum functions. These are families of men of high salaries or of men who have developed fairly large enterprises but who never themselves inherited lineage or money. These families revolve around the career of the husband, and they are concerned with the cultivation of a taste in clothes, wines, interior decoration, and entertainment. Clubs and committees are often necessities for these men. So are cooperative wives who create a home to which they can invite friends with some pride and who help them with contacts in the community which will be useful to their careers. These families often gravitate towards art centers. They do so because they are capable of enjoying art, and also because they recognize that art is a status symbol. Besides, they can thus associate with the élite. One respondent enjoyed the openings and similar events at the Museum because, he said, the Museum was "introducing the Governor and things like that." All these seem to constitute a strongly motivated audience that one can count upon.

The small businessmen and the semiprofessionals of the lower middle class also want to be upwardly mobile, yet most of them will not rise very far, and quite a large number of them seem willing to admit, at least in intimate conversation, that they are going to remain where they are. They stress their respectability; they own their own homes in most cases; they are morally strict and

143

more churchgoing than any other segment of society; and they want careers for their children and are anxious to send them to college. Among this group of people are some intermittent Museum and theatregoers. "I do like to go to the Museum," said one. "It is like going to a rich house. It is awe-inspiring." They do not seem to consider their Museum visit as "enjoyment" but rather as "education." When they go, they like to take their children. "We're interested in doing everything for the children and keeping up with culture for them," said a mother about a visit to the Museum.

In the working class there is an upper segment of semiskilled operatives who work from day to day and live adequately but on small margins. Their jobs are not so financially and psychologically rewarding as are those of the middle class. Their satisfactions by and large seem to come from activities outside work: family gatherings, weekends, vacations. Here is a large group of persons concerned constantly with non-work gratifications who rarely seem to find their way to the Museum or theatre. They often say "it costs too much."

Finally, there is a lower segment of the working class, mostly immigrant or Negro, with large families living in slums, who are often employed only in temporary jobs. Apathetic or preoccupied with sheer physical survival, they cannot realistically be considered a potentially significant audience for fine arts. The entire working class composes approximately one-half of the population of the Museum town.

Interest in and visits to the Museum decline as we descend the ladder of money, power, and education. However, knowledge about the Museum and its activities declines as well. The call from the Museum is heard less often in the lower classes; one laborer interviewed did not know that the Museum existed.

B. The *opportunities to attend* the Museum exhibits are generally restricted to the daytime. (Exhibits may occasionally be opened at night at the time when other Museum functions, such as art lectures, are scheduled, so that the audience of such special functions can also enjoy the galleries.) This, of course, restricts the weekday audiences to those who are not employed, predominantly women, children, retired persons, and tourists.

The tourist group is not without interest. Some conversations with middle- and working-class persons indicate that local patriotism, or pride in "our town," frequently determines their attitude towards museums and theatres. When relatives or friends from other parts of the country come visiting they are taken to such showplaces. This is accepted as normal by both hosts and visitors, even though they otherwise would not go to the museum or theatre. It is virtually a part of being a good tourist and a good host to do this. A lower-class woman expressed it this way: "You know any time any-

body goes to the city you always go to the Museum."
She offered this also as an explanation of her visits to
several out-of-town galleries. The hosts are rewarded
with a sense of pride for living in a community with
such facilities, and the guests accept the museum or theatre visit somewhat in the same vein as a sticker for their
car which shows they have been in this sightseeing spot
or that. Attendance at art centers may thus be expected
to fluctuate according to the rate of the tourist trade.

C. The greater the *variety of offerings* of the Museum, the greater is the chance that a person will find
something to his taste, and that he will attend. The Museum has indeed a variety of offerings, more than museums in cities of comparable size usually have. One may
doubt that further diversification of the art program
will aid attendance to a worth-while extent, given the
present size of the art-interested public reached by the
galleries. The Museum Theatre can diversify its offering by presenting more modern plays. It must be remembered that the diversification of the offerings has
been the recent history of the Museum, and that the
directors feel that attendance rates have not been commensurate with the cost and effort to provide the expanded collection and repertoire.

In sum, our theory when confronted with the situation of the Museum suggests that the public's response
is small because the population reached by the call from

the Museum is small—primarily the higher strata in a middle-size town—and the opportunities for this population to attend are limited by the Museum schedule.

The Museum in the Artistic Reward System

One variety of programming at the Museum should be specially mentioned. The galleries during the season have generally three exhibits: (1) the permanent collection of the Museum, (2) a temporary exhibit, usually on loan from elsewhere, and (3) an exhibit of local artists from the state served by the Museum. The latter is the smallest of the exhibits—a handful of paintings or sculptures—and least conspicuously placed in the galleries. However, it does remind us of something our theory noted in passing:

> For a contemporary painter, . . . [the reward pattern] would include the number of private shows, the number and kinds of reviews by critics, the rating of the galleries in which his paintings have been exhibited, the number and prominence of the collectors who have acquired paintings, the number of paintings hanging in museums, et cetera (*supra,* p. 114).

It is clear that the Museum, like other galleries, administers great honorific rewards to artists by arranging for large or small, one-man or group exhibitions. These

147

have considerable bearing also on the artists' financial rewards, since they tend to set the price level at which he can market his pictures. Outsiders are often surprised at how important such occasions may be to artists or actors, who generally agree as to what exhibition halls and stages outrank others. The artists and actors are ego-involved, sometimes profoundly, in the arrangements and the "billings" which make their names visible to the world. "I had my pictures hung there at the Museum last year," said one painter. "I loved the staging of that. My name was up in woodblock. My pictures were on stands. There was a biography of me. It was all kept simple, and it was great to have my pictures there."

The directors of galleries, theatres, and publishing houses are thus often perceived by the artists to be in a position of controlling the very fundamental gratifications of giving or denying fame. The ways in which they administer these rewards are watched carefully and subjected to endless discussions among the artists. Artists and actors in the Museum town who look to the Museum and its Museum Theatre as administrators of cherished rewards, have much to say as to how the Museum uses its resources to promote their fame. Most of it is critical. One remarked: "You have probably seen the funny little cubicle in which they squeeze [state] artists, while they obviously can spend fantastic sums on an exhibition on theatre design which is after all something rather special. And they have a very elaborate design for any exhibit. It does perhaps increase the enjoyment, but in a way a good exhibit should be able to stand by itself, and we feel that all that money might have been spent on something else [i.e., promotion of the contemporary art 'we' stand for]." And one informant familiar with young artists reports that the "art students just hate it, the waste, all the bowing and scraping, their trying to impress falsely and making art something costly —and it should be living around us." A third artist, however, volunteered a different viewpoint: "Another thing the artists complain about is that they don't get enough space at the Museum. It strikes me as a small amount of narcissism, because not all of art in this state is on such a high level."

The attitude of the local actors to the Museum Theatre parallels in part the attitude of the local artists to the Museum galleries. We have observed the eagerness to appear in a play at the Museum Theatre: "I just couldn't be more thrilled than when I am working there," said one actress. "The Museum Theatre is tops in any respect," said another. On the other hand, there is much resentment against the Museum for its present policy of denying its facilities to other theatre groups in the state. "The other theatre groups want to use the Museum Theatre. They think the policy of the Museum is stingy." "What would be wonderful, just a dream come true, would be if those scrumptious facilities could be booked by theatre groups around the town."

In the view of the artists and actors there is also another element than the feeling that the Museum denies them rewards it is capable of giving. Any museum, by its mere existence and prestige and by its educational activities in the community, is a formidable creator of taste through the promotion of art events. The artist perceives the museum as able to increase the market for art simply by increasing the public's general interest in art. Most museums, however, are largely showplaces for "old objects of art," and they display relatively few modern pieces. A museum may thus promote a taste different from that manifested in the works of most local artists. (One of the artists who talked to us suggested somewhat bitterly that "the Museum seems to favor rococo.") Consequently, artists often feel that museums direct the taste of the local market away from *their* art. This may account for some of the hostility directed against museums or for the ambivalent attitudes among groups of artists.

At any rate, there is no doubt that we deal with a situation in which the practicing artists are resentful of an art organization for its role in the artistic reward pattern. The Museum is considered somewhat less than generous in according local artists the honorific rewards it controls.

150

Art and the Integration of the Élite

It is generally felt that art is an institutional realm that lacks clear-cut stratification. The common use of phrases such as "it is merely a matter of taste," or "why quarrel about taste," attests to the fact that our society does not impose rigid scales for measuring tastes. While some tastes are recognized as better than others, the amount of leeway between the ugly and the beautiful is great indeed. Our theory has an interesting point to make about this phenomenon of fuzzy stratification of an institutional value—

It appears that the presence of an institutional realm that lacks clear-cut stratification facilitates interaction between people with positions in more stratified institutional realms. For instance, a religion that does not allow much of the "I am holier than thou" sentiment may serve as a meeting ground where people of different ranks in economy, polity and science can get together with some sense of equality. Such a religion serves as an integrative force in society (*supra,* p. 118).

An application of these ideas from the realm of religion to the realm of art can be quite suggestive. Compared with the effort necessary to gain money, power, or scholarly competence in today's society, taste (or rather, the appearance of taste) is acquired with relative ease. Money, power, and academic competence cannot easily be acquired simultaneously, although one can acquire money and, at the same time, good taste; or power and taste; or academic honor and taste. This means, then, that most persons who hold or achieve élite positions can acquire a taste which may not be perfect but which may yet be (or appear to be) well-developed.

Shared taste makes it easier for people to like and enjoy each other. There is much evidence in everyday life of mutual attraction of persons who have common esthetic reactions. Leaders committed to different organizations attract each other because they enjoy the same art styles. They may be different in other respects: one may be a lawyer, one a businessman, one a physician, one a college professor, one a clergyman, one an engineer. Their common taste creates their attraction for each other, and this attraction is one source of the integration of the élite by which a society achieves direction and perpetuates itself. Thus, it turns out that in our society art is more than decorative; it also reinforces societal life.

One should not assume that the creators and consumers of art are aware, as individuals, of the societal consequence of their involvement in art. Once brought to our attention, however, it is easy to document the phenomenon that in practice many art activities constitute precisely an integration of the élite. One trustee of the Museum said, as a matter of course: "The Museum should be used by educators, clergymen, bankers, and others [of their kind]." Every American art museum or symphony we know about seems to have its inner circle of community leaders who are its patrons, contributors, or volunteers. They meet semiprivately at openings, celebrations, or art events of one kind or another. They naturally exchange views about the art exhibited or the performance they have seen and thus reveal their taste preferences. This preference was fairly homogeneous to begin with, and the exchange of comments makes it even more so, according to the principle of convergence (*supra,* p. 81). In all, common taste is a bond among them. But also, and invariably, they discuss other matters that concern them.

Here we can observe men and women in command of wealth, power, knowledge, or reverence formulating their agreement on vital issues, such as matters of finance or material acquisitions; and they exchange opinions about other persons with whom they may become associated through marriage, business, or politics. At gatherings in the Museum we overheard remarks such as these: "The Governor told me last week that he would not push [that] legislation this session." "If you believe your Board will accept, let's have the lawyers draw up the deed." "P. is a good man and I've known

153

him for years. I think you can trust him with the job."
"Oh, dear, the M's are such a fine family, friends of
H's." It would be unfair and unwise to dismiss this as
gossip. Much of it is vital communication necessary for
the functioning of the community. In view of this, it is
natural that the president of a large business enterprise
in the museum town would say: "On the openings I
always enjoy going as much for the Museum itself as for
the social attraction. There is a special kind of people
there on special occasions." Similar sentiments were expressed by persons whose main commitments are to politics and to science.[1]

It should be noted that it is almost a professional ne-

---

1 It is implicit in art events which serve as a meeting ground for the
élite that the participants have some degree of taste, and this could be
the source of an interesting conflict. An art center as a rule is run by
a professional staff striving for perfection in taste. The élite who need
the art center for the contacts it provides may not want to make all
the effort required to refine their own tastes. Thus, they occasionally
press for a more modest level of sophistication in the art events that
bring them together. A businessman, not at all without culture, who
is very anxious to attend showings and theatre openings for their
artistic, but more important, their social significance, raises a protest
against the perfectionist: "When you are frustrated all day by business,
you want to get to a light show in the evenings." This man seems to
be willing to exert pressure, through friends who serve on the Board
of Trustees, for a more popular taste level. The professionals of the art
centers meet this challenge by trying to educate their audience through
lectures and courses. However, according to the principle of the limit
of actions (*supra*, p. 74) this advanced art education does not necessarily
reach the men who are busy with the economy, government, science,
and religion of the community. Its effects seem greatest on groups which
have more leisure time.

154

cessity for museum directors and curators to co-operate with the very rich, or at least to keep on good terms with them. A large number of art objects that come to a museum has been bought, not just with rich people's money but at no or little cost for the rich donor, with money that otherwise would have gone to the tax collector. Suppose a museum curator can co-operate with a man in a 90 per cent tax bracket and advise him about the purchase of an art painting that will meet the need of his museum. The purchaser puts it in his home for a few years and then has it appraised, usually finding that it has appreciated some 10 to 15 per cent. He donates it to the museum, a non-profit educational organization, and claims the appreciated value as a charitable tax deduction. His income tax is then reduced roughly with the cost of the painting. In effect, the whole transaction tied up some capital but cost him little or nothing, except some paper work for his lawyer and accountant, and he had the enjoyment of the picture in his home for the intervening years. This unwitting way, in which the government through its tax laws subsidizes art, has many ramifications. Here it is enough to note one: Museum directors do well if they stay on good terms with the economic élite, not just for short periods of fund raising drives but for the extended periods that these transactions involve.

The attraction that art has for the élite and the efforts

of museum curators to stay on good terms with the élite means that the art exhibition or stage event is likely to resemble a gathering of privileged families. Articulate but soft-spoken men and women of ease seem to dominate at these gatherings. A woman described her first encounter with the inner circle in the Museum in the following words: "It was a very aristocratic, dignified, prestigey, down-the-nosish evening. I half-way love that sort of thing anyway, with all the sophisticated clothes and all." We can observe at a glance that the style of life prevailing among the élite is likely to prevail at art and play openings.

It is this style in social intercourse which sets apart the marginal group, those who do not "belong" from the élite. "Of course, you feel like a peasant, and you're kind of glad you're probably as well dressed and behaved as anyone there so that the peasantness doesn't come through," said one woman who isn't sure whether she belongs or not but who manages to disguise her insecurity. In answering questions on Museum membership, she said: "Aside from us teachers, mostly their members are . . . society people. They have more than middle-class money. They have more time than working people have. Lots of big names. That's most of the atmosphere. In fact . . . the whole place just breathes money. It's just not a natural habitat for people like me. . . . Except for the Theatre, I'm really not too comfortable there." And the response of outsiders has been even less happy. Thus we see not only that art consumption helps to integrate the élite, but also that the style of life that the élite bring to art events in a subtle way discourages participation by the non-élite.

Let us now sum up our second application of theoretical principles to the client's problem, and say that we deal with a situation in which various institutional élites interact as equals (or near equals) in one institutional realm with unclear stratification (art), but that they bring to this interaction many attributes of stratified institutional realms (economy, polity, science) so that the non-élite is alienated.

Art and the Circulation of Economic and Political Élites

We know that art is an "institutional realm," beauty is its "institutional value," and taste is its "mode of stratification" (see *supra,* pp. 68–70). Our theory contains several propositions about these general phenomena. For example:

Those who experience a rise in their control of one institutional value, are likely to feel a certain pressure to acquire control of other institutional values as well. Thus, it happens that the modes of stratification in various institutional realms tend to cluster. Those who rank high in terms of one want to become high in others as well (*supra,* pp. 115–116).

Applied to our problem, this means that those who are rising in the worlds of money, power, and knowledge want to rise in taste as well. The man who achieves prosperity, power, or academic honor begins to want beauty as well. Such upwardly mobile people are hence attracted to a museum—a promising lead for our thinking.

However, our theoretical knowledge, supported by observations by almost anybody interested in the human drama, indicates that some frustrations are likely in this process. As one art instructor remarked about the art public in the museum town: "There are some types of persons who've suddenly started earning money and they start pretending that they are upper crust. Of course, they don't fool anybody but themselves." The *nouveau riche,* or the *parvenu* in power, discovers that his new peers appreciate a style of art different from that popular in the group he has left. He is naturally influenced by his new group (*supra,* p. 81) and may even be anxious to be accepted in his new stratum and to acquire all its paraphernalia, to "start pretending to be upper crust." He is apt to select and exaggerate the most visible and conspicuous aspects of his new position and becomes "ostentatious" and "vulgar" compared

with those who are, in a sense, to the manner born. It is also likely that an established élite could insist on subtle refinements in taste—adding *U*'s to their scale of evaluation our theory would say (*supra,* p. 92)—to draw more lines between themselves and the *nouveau riche* or the *parvenu.* At any rate, the climbers are not allowed to "fool anybody but themselves."

We also know from our theory that people are apt to make visible their more favorable attributes and play down less favorable ones (*supra,* p. 87). Thus, when some families of the old élite fail to hold the same prominent place as their ancestors, their claim on society is more frequently phrased not in terms of their own deeds, but in terms of those of the past. They take special delight in antiques and in art styles of an earlier and more illustrious period. Oriented toward the past, they eschew modern art, which represents to them "our degenerate times," that is, the times in which their families are no longer quite as important and quite as secure as they once were. Only those families who can enjoy contemporary fame, power, and riches as well as ancestors of great prominence are likely to comfortably encompass both traditional and modern art styles. By birth they have the traditions, and they are secure enough to experiment with novel ideas. The men and women who control the Museum mostly belong to this established élite, or to a declining élite.

In sum, this last application of theory to the problem of the client suggests this: We deal with a situation in which a rising economic and political élite wants help in acquiring a taste commensurate with its new élite status from an art organization (the Museum) which is largely controlled by an established or declining élite reluctant to admit the rising élite as equals.

Confronting the Client with a Scholarly Understanding of His Situation

The picture of the Museum and its problem, pieced together with the help of theoretical principles, was presented to the client; the presentation was first done piecemeal in conversation, and then comprehensively in writing as part of the final report.

A confrontation of this kind points up both the advantage and the futility of applied social theory. After a few days or weeks, the consultant is expected to tell the client something about a problem that the client has known first-hand for years or decades. What the consultant can offer at this point is not so much previously unknown facts but previously unknown *relations* between facts. It would be both pretentious and false to suggest that the Museum director did not know the facts that entered the consultant's review of his situation. But it is not wrong to suggest that many of these facts appeared in what is usually called "a new light," that is, in new relations to each other.[2] This is the main service to the client of the scholarly confrontation. The commonplace is re-examined in view of its not-so-commonplace causes and consequences brought to the fore by the consultant. Familiar events again begin to arouse the client's curiosity, and routine ways of doing things do not appear as self-evident as before.

Often the client can take over from here. The new perspective he has gained is more valuable to him than the specific advice the consultant has not yet given.

The Museum clients graciously acknowledged that their confrontation with the sociological picture of their operations gave them new ideas. Yet conversation revealed also the partial nature of the scholarly understanding that was achieved. The consultant had nothing to say when asked two pertinent questions:

Do people like what they see in our Museum and the way it is arranged?

Do the many educational activities that the Museum has for school children help them to grow up as regular museum goers?

These questions represent, of course, the established ways of the Museum to get visitors: to have a fine col-

2 *Cf.* the discussion of the "Overlooked Variable" in Robert K. Merton, "The Role of Applied Social Science in the Formation of Policy," *Philosophy of Science*, XVI (1949), pp. 178–179. See also, *supra,* p. 64.

lection attractively displayed, and to teach the growing generation the beauty and enjoyment of the art shown. The plain circumstance is that nothing in theoretical sociology could be relevantly related to these issues. All that could be done was to formulate some questions by means of information gleaned in the exploratory study. This was done in the written report, which made these points:

The Museum Visit. The occasional and incidental museum or theatre visitor seems to have some problems that are not readily understood by the regular visitors or the professional staff. To put it simply, he does not know how to behave in the art gallery or theatre. Certain visible rules prevail in an art gallery or theatre: "Do not smoke," "Do not touch," or "This way out." But there are others not so obvious to an outsider. They remain implicit and the outsider or incidental visitor consequently remains more or less uncertain about them. For example, we generally expect a museum visitor to conform to expectations: "Do not talk loudly," "Do not laugh," "Keep a serious but relaxed expression on your face," "Show in your behavior a certain deference," "Behave as if you realize that the Museum is not any ordinary place," "Don't give the staff a feeling that their efforts are in vain," "Pay due attention to objects recognized as outstanding," "Don't walk too fast—that under-

162

mines morale," "Don't walk too slowly—that gives others guilt feelings," "Don't stand too close to others," "Don't watch others too closely while they look at something," etc. These and many other informal norms are uncertain or unknown to the incidental visitor. He may feel uncomfortable and insecure as a result, and anxiously seek hints from the guards and fellow visitors. The role imputed to the guards in such dilemmas is a curious one. One of the visitors we spoke to exclaimed: "I wouldn't dare parade there with my kids. If they broke some treasure I'd just die. The discipline there is terrific. For adults, too, I mean. Every time I think of the Museum I hear the guard's voice, 'Don't touch that, miss.' Every time I have gone I have felt watched like a hawk." When the number of visitors is small, the guards are more noticeable and each visitor thus feels himself under closer scrutiny. On crowded days the incidental and inexperienced visitor might feel more comfortable since he then can follow the average behavior of the crowd. The theatre or concert visit can always give the unsophisticated the comfort of doing as others do. Nevertheless, one working-class man reported that he and his wife were ill at ease during their first theatre visit. They did not know when to applaud or what to do in the intermission: "It wasn't like the movies where you can sit and hold her hand."

When it comes right down to it, we know very little

about what goes on when art is "appreciated." We know from other studies that one listens to the radio as a rule when alone; that families watch television together; that preferably one goes to the movies with friends or peers. We might guess that most theatre visits are made in company, and this may also be true of museum visits. But the group-dynamics of art consumption has never been studied.

Art Education in the Museum. Museums and similar organizations spend much time and energy educating children in art appreciation, for to them the children represent the future audience. By liaison and co-operation with the schools, museum officials hope, among other things, to train a future generation of more loyal museum-goers and art-lovers. Such assumptions of returns for investments seem reasonable enough. It should be pointed out, however, that we have no firm evidence whatsoever that existing educational programs are actually accomplishing this.

It may well be that art education in school does create a genuine desire for art understanding and need of art experiences. However, here as elsewhere, the presence of an honest and recognized *need* does not necessarily mean that a person will *act* upon it. A woman may honestly want to lose weight and this may be a very strong need of hers. However, spending most of her time in the kitchen and at luncheons and teas does not give her

164

many environmental openings to do what she wants. Likewise, a boy or a girl from the working class or lower middle class may acquire a real desire for fine arts in school, but his or her daily milieu may be virtually void of opportunities to view fine arts and instead be full of television shows, cheap movies, comic strips, and popular magazines. If he or she does not grow up to be a museum enthusiast we can hardly put the blame on inadequate art education during the school years.

Possibly the educational programs of museums have also had some unintended consequences. The idea might develop, for example, that one grows out of museum visits in the same way one grows out of school. How else can we understand the working-class man who, when asked whether he had gone to the Museum, answered: "Oh, no, not me. The Museum is fine for the kids." The public's image of the Museum in society may be distorted as a result of the recent emphasis on educational activities. Since a museum is so closely linked with education, the decision to make a visit may entail a greater effort than otherwise in the minds of many people: They may resist the idea because it sounds like "work," which is very different from "enjoyment." How widespread such sentiments are only further study can tell.

These two problems—the drama of a museum visit

and the effect of art education—cannot be brought any closer to solution by confronting them with existing social theory; at least this was impossible in the present instance. They became instead problems for research. A series of participant observations and experiments can be designed to reveal just what goes on before, during, and after a museum visit, and a survey can be made to find out whether those whose school classes went to the museums and theatres fifteen years ago today make up a larger share of art owners or audiences than do those whose schools fifteen years ago did not have any such program.

The moral of the above is simple: A consultant may and probably should recommend research studies on problems that do not lend themselves to a scholarly understanding through linkage with existing theory.[3]

Calculation of Solutions

One of our theorems said that "the larger the population reached by the market call of an offering, the great-

[3] This principle was poorly understood at the time of the Museum consultation (*cf. infra,* p. 188). The Bureau of Applied Social Research under whose auspices the work was done also wanted research studies designed of the several problems (*supra,* pp. 140–160) for which a scholarly understanding had been achieved on the basis of already existing knowledge. However, the Museum rejected all proposals for further research, both the general ones designed to confirm the scholarly understanding obtained and the ones on the drama of the museum visit and the effects of art education.

er is the market response" (*supra,* p. 103). Applied to our problem this reads: the larger the population the Museum can reach with its announcements, the more people will attend (*supra,* pp. 141–145). Two solutions follow:

(S 1) *If the Museum moves to a larger city, it will have better attendance.* This would apply also to specific shows or plays originating in the Museum. If they are presented in larger cities, given the same amount of advertising and a similar Museum setting, they would draw larger audiences than in the home town.

(S 2) *If the Museum increases the number of persons reached by its announcements it would increase attendance.* Our understanding is that the upper class and upper middle class is at present well reached. This solution would apply to the lower middle class and the working class.

Another of our theorems said that "the greater the number of opportunities available to a population to heed a market call, the greater is its response" (*supra,* p. 105). Applied to the Museum this would read: the more opportunities there are to attend Museum functions the more people will attend (*supra,* pp. 145–146). Or,

(S 3) *If the Museum functions were scheduled at times when more opportunities exist for people to attend, attendance would increase.* We understand that the present hours do not provide ample opportunities for people employed during regular work hours.

The third of our market response theorems said: "The greater the variety of offerings in a market call the greater the response" (*supra,* p. 105), or in terms of our problem: The greater the variety of programs and services offered by the Museum the greater the attendance (*supra,* p. 146). Thus we have:

(S 4) *If the programs of the Museum were more diversified, attendance would increase.* We understood, however, that the Museum already has a diversified gallery exhibit and lectures and that further diversification would affect mostly the Museum Theatre.

We noted that the negative attitude toward the Museum held by artists on account of the less generous role played by the Museum in their reward system (*supra,* pp. 147–150). Our theory states that "influentials have more knowledge than their imitators" (*supra,* p. 82). Now artists have more knowledge of art than laymen, and it follows that the artists are "influentials" among the general public in matters concerning the Museum. Thus we arrive at an important conclusion: If the artists in the population served by the Museum had a more favorable opinion about the Museum, a larger segment of the population would also have a more favorable opinion about the Museum. We know further from our theory that "persons tend to embrace new opinions

168

and engage in new actions that are consonant with their past communications and actions" (*supra,* p. 99). This, of course, applies also to the action of attending the Museum. Thus, if local artists had a more favorable opinion of the Museum, public attendance would increase. (Note that this does not simply mean that more artists will attend, but also the many more persons who look to artists as influentials in matters of art.) Since the more or less favorable opinion of the artists is dependent on the more or less generous and judicious use of artistic rewards controlled by the Museum, we may say:

(S 5) *If the Museum were more judicious and generous in allocating (honorific) rewards to local artists, public attendance would increase.*

Finally, let us contrast what our theory says about equalitarian relations with our understanding that visitors bring to the Museum gatherings attributes of stratified institutional realms. The theory says: "From time to time most superiors give up the deference of their high position to enjoy the fun and joy of play with equals and if left alone, inferiors are likely to turn work into play to share its joy. However, the fun is not forever; it disappears as soon as someone fails to act as an equal, or as soon as someone makes a tactless remark that makes the participants aware of their differences in riches, power, holiness, education, taste, or virtue" (*supra,* pp. 117–118). Plainly, the many visible symbols of

169

community standing displayed at Museum gatherings may get in the way of the simple enjoyment of communion with equals. Assuming as before that this enjoyment and attendance are related, we may say:

(S 6) *If the participants at Museum gatherings were to make the symbols of their membership in economic and political élite less visible, the attendance would increase.*

Presenting Practical Advice

Each of the calculated solutions has the general formulation, "If X, then better attendance." To turn such sentences into advice we accept the client's value premise that increased attendance is all to the good and transform the sentences into "Do X." But we also use our knowledge of the client's situation to give as many concrete references to X as we can. The advice must not be abstract, it must be concrete.

Furthermore, it is not much use to present advice that tells the client to change matters that are beyond his power. Take, for example, (S 1): "If the Museum moves to a larger city, it will have better attendance." However, the recommendation "Move the Museum to a larger city" is unrealistic. The Museum has a charter to serve the people of the state and is located in the largest city in the state. To ask it to move to a bigger city is to ask the impossible. Such advice, although a formally correct solution to the attendance problem, is never presented to the client. The general rule is: Do not give recommendations requiring change in things beyond the client's control. Of the solutions we calculated, (S 1) is the only one that leads to this kind of unrealistic advice. The others have realistic implications.

(S 2) If the Museum increases the number of persons reached by its announcements it would increase attendance.

As mentioned, this applies best to the lower middle class and the working classes; those better off are already sufficiently informed. Experience shows that television is by far the most effective medium to reach these groups. Spot local television announcements should perhaps be tried to announce the most important events of the year at the Museum. Direct mail to these large population segments is expensive and out of all question, but one can easily acquire the membership lists of a civic group like the Elks and veterans groups like the American Legion which have extensive representation in these strata. Members in these and similar groups should be put on the Museum mailing list. Or, perhaps these groups can be persuaded to enclose a folder from the Museum in their own mailings to members.

(S 3) If the Museum functions were scheduled at

times when more opportunities exist for people to attend, attendance would increase.

As mentioned, present opening hours make it hard for those who work during the day to attend. Hold the Museum open at night and on weekends! Since this is a very common idea in any discussion of Museum attendance, let us merely note that it is a sociologically sound one. To keep budgets for guards and attendance in balance, this recommendation usually is supplemented by the recommendation to keep museums closed during the morning hours, when there is a relatively low attendance.

(S 4) If the programs of the Museum were more diversified, attendance would increase.

Diversity can be achieved in many ways, for example by adding painting classes and special exhibitions for children. However, since exhibits already are very diversified, this applies mostly to the theatre. Get some more variety into the repertoire! The fact that a play was written in this century or even this decade should not make it harder for it to get performed at the Museum Theatre. The theatre may also be used for a larger variety of films of artistic merit. Of course, diversification of services can be carried out much beyond this: a restaurant, a branch of the public library, a nursery, and many more services might be added to the Museum. While they would certainly increase attendance, we shall not consider them since they are not central to fine arts.

(S 5) If the Museum were more judicious and generous in allocating honorific rewards to local artists, public attendance would increase.

The reasoning that led to this solution was complex, and it does not follow from the scholarly understanding reported earlier. This solution can, however, be easily grasped with the help of illustrations from our exploratory study. Our cue comes from a large number of studies which tell us that the decision making of the public takes place most often in a network of personal interrelations. Decisions to vote, to buy, to contribute, to participate in an event are rarely simple responses to appeals made in newspapers, over the radio or television, or through the mail. They are made in discussions with others; people sound each other out in cliques; and many may never have heard or seen the original appeal. In these informal groups there are usually one or more "influentials" from whom the others take their cues. Some opinion leaders are on an equal status level with their followers; some are on a higher status level; and most have *more knowledge* about the matter at hand. There is no reason to assume that decisions about participation in art events are made differently. The persons who are *most* influential in the general public's decision to attend art and theatre events may often be the artists and actors and similar

173

persons because they have superior knowledge about the event. If they say the event is "dull" or "stuffy," their opinion followers are not likely to attend. Anything the art center does to alienate or to arouse resentment among the community of artists and actors, may be compounded. Not only will these groups shun the event themselves, but their more numerous opinion followers will likely do so too. For example, if we assume that each of the five hundred actors in the area is the influential among five friends, workmates, relatives, or acquaintances, then they and their followers constitute a potential theatre audience of fifteen hundred to two thousand—allowing for duplication—enough to make up the deficit on almost any production at the Museum Theatre.

One of our respondents who had appeared in a Museum performance said about his own visits to the Theatre: "Usually I make a point of going with friends who would not go otherwise. . . . I try to introduce people to the Theatre and we make it an enjoyable and uplifting event." The fact that most performances at the Museum Theatre are in part, at least, *amateur* performances may also bring new people to the audience. They come out of loyalty to neighbors or friends, or out of mere curiosity to see a person they may know in everyday life in a new and strange setting. One amateur actor said: "You always go to see somebody you know.

At least thirty people came to see me." A leader in one of the other theatre groups in the city explained to us how he quite consciously served as one influential. "Theatre attendance in [this town] is due to somebody grabbing you by the collar and saying, 'Let's go see this tonight.' My own group, they'd never attended live theatre. Then I got mixed up in the ———— Theatre. My wife and I would call up friends and say, 'How about going to the show?' And before they could say no, say, 'And stop by our house for a drink afterward.' . . . You need some gimmick. People are not apt to come for live theatre itself—there's usually some ulterior motive. You first get audiences out for some loyalty, friendship or some promotional gimmick," he continued. "But if they enjoy themselves, they'll do all right. We see our audiences growing steadily." Likewise, the several hundred artists in the Museum town, plus their opinion followers, might make any exhibition a success in attendance. And each new visitor might add to attendance figures even further because of the likelihood of "chain reactions," that is, some opinion followers of a participant are, in turn, influentials in other circles.

Against this background, the fact that most local artists and many actors harbor resentments against the Museum's role in their reward pattern (*supra,* pp. 147–150) becomes of consequence. To win these local talents over to a more enthusiastic view of the Museum would have a multiplier effect on the audience. Thus we recommend: Enlarge the space and attention given by the Museum to local talents in the fine arts. Give more staff time to them, and allow them representation in the various groups in the Museum that affect policy. Use the publicity machinery possessed by the Museum to make local talents known to the general public. Of course, better artists should be given the more publicity and exhibition space than less good ones, but in case of doubt about the merits of a local talent make it a rule to err on the generous rather than the stingy side.

(S 6) If the participants at Museum gatherings were to make the symbols of their membership in economic and political élites less visible, attendance would increase.

Dinner jackets, jewelry, and forms of address revealing status should be played down at Museum lectures and openings, and perhaps even at theatre evenings. How this is to be accomplished we cannot say, but some prominent hostesses should be asked to take the lead in making those less accustomed to the glitters of the world feel more at home.

Complications

Let us for the time being accept that the consultant has reasoned right from right premises and indeed reached the right solutions. We thus assume that if his advice is followed, attendance at the Museum will increase. There remains one more thing to do before leaving the client to implement the solutions. We have to consider possible *additional* consequences, apart from increased attendance, that flow from the proposed solutions. Such consequences are known as "complications," and they may be welcome or they may be unwanted. Two complications can easily be detected in the solutions proposed for the Museum.

1. If more of the resources of the Museum are given to promote local art, then exhibition space, staff time, and the like are taken from the promotion of the national and international art. Since the latter is almost always better than local art, this means that the Museum is compromising its basic objective to display the most beautiful art.

2. If attendance is increased through these measures, the Museum and its gatherings will be much less of an exclusive meeting ground for the élite. The rather latent, but highly useful, function performed by the Museum in integrating the élite will then be difficult to maintain and may be lost entirely. This may not be desirable.

In view of such complications, decisions to implement the suggested solutions do not become as easy as they appeared at first. Like so many human decisions they

177

are shown to involve priorities and value commitments, both latent and manifest. A consultation can only help a client to a scholarly understanding of his situation and it can give him useful ideas for solutions. But a consultation is not meant to remove the necessity for making decisions, nor the agony and anguish in making them.

5 On the Uses of Consultations

The practitioners of applied social science, be they researchers or consultants, soon find that their trade involves them in a variety of human dramas, and that success in delivering the correct scientific solution bears a tenuous relation to success from the point of view of the client. A whole book could be written about this; I will only deal with some aspects that are not generally emphasized.[1]

---

[1] *Cf.* Gunnar Myrdal, "The Relation between Social Theory and Social Policy," *British Journal of Sociology*, IV (1953), pp. 210–242, and Alvin W. Gouldner, "Theoretical Requirements of the Applied Social Sciences," *American Sociological Review*, Vol. XXII (1957), pp. 92–102.

Abuses of Applied Science

A researcher or consultant may be called into a conflict situation by one of the parties in the conflict, merely to embarrass the opponent. This is not a bad weapon in a fight within an organization: To induce a researcher to go and ask for access to an opponent's files and to send his interviewers around asking probing questions in the opponent's division can be very nerve-racking and helps break down the opponent's spirit to fight. In a less Machiavellian way, a call for research is also a call for postponement of an adverse or unpleasant decision.

Moreover, a social scientist is often called in when for all practical purposes a big decision has already been made. The executives who made the decision are naturally somewhat anxious, since it involves large sums of money and the welfare of many men. In this situation, research or consultation may serve as an anxiety-reducing ritual. It functions somewhat as a wedding ceremony does for many who get married. The minister asks if the man wants this woman for better or worse. The man's answer to this anxiety-provoking question has already been decided. However, it is not a useless ritual. After the ritual the man and the woman do the same things they did before, but they feel more comfortable about it. Likewise the executives who made the big decision feel more comfortable about it after the research ritual. And the ritual had some good side effects. The fact that it was done alerted many people to the fact that a change was in the offing—just as the wedding ceremony signaled a change of someone's marital status to the larger community. The fact that it caused people to discuss and talk over a problem might have generated a much needed consensus among those affected—just as the wedding ceremony usually ends the controversy as to whether the parties are well suited to each other. Also—and this should never be overlooked by a researcher or consultant—consciously or unconsciously the research or consultation ritual establishes a scapegoat should the decision prove to be disastrous. Then the executives can tell their inquiring board or investigating subcommittee: "Look, we did the best we could and had the best advice. We even spent X dollars on consultation and research."

Research or consultation done under these circumstances is not meant to be used in policy decisions. But it would be interesting to know how much such research goes on.

Some Prerequisites for Successful Use of Applied Science

Even when applied research or consultation is contracted in earnest, and any failure to use it cannot be

181

blamed on the inability of the decision maker to manipulate the variables dealt with by the scientist, many
problems remain. It is a rather common observation
that the scientific findings do not by themselves influence any policy decision; it is always *findings plus something else* that seem to be operative in any instance
where it is claimed that applied science has helped the
shaping of a policy. From the case studies of utilization
of social science that we have encountered it should be
possible to compile a list of factors that constitute this
"something else" which has to be present if findings
shall be of any use. Unfortunately, one searches the literature in vain for publications containing case histories
of applied social science and its actual uses.[2]

The generalizations one can make are thus tentative.
However, from the stories that have drifted my way
about used and unused research or consultation reports,
one simple feature stands out: Applied social science is
most likely to be used when there is *a habit of co-operation between scientist and executive.*

Co-operation implies, of course, some consensus on
goals and adequate communication. When scientist and
client embrace opposite goals and when they do not talk
each other's language, the research results or consulta-

---

[2] The Bureau of Applied Social Research at Columbia University has
announced that it will compile such a case book from its rich files, but
so far nothing has appeared in print.

tion reports are likely to remain unused in a file drawer. Applied research and consultation are always geared to the client's goal; if the scientist cannot accept this goal as worthwhile he is likely to produce a report of limited use to the client. (The right thing for the scientist to do in this dilemma is to decline the assignment, not only on account of the limited use his results face, but simply on account of personal happiness and sense of integrity.)

Applied science, furthermore, must always present findings in the client's language. The researcher who cannot present his results in anything but the technical vocabulary of his science—and technical sociology can be quite technical—cannot expect to see his findings put to use by men of action who talk and understand a common-sense language. Only when there is a history of long co-operation do executives begin to use and understand technical terms; for example, many modern businessmen are well versed in the technical language of academic economics.

Consensus on goals and a common language, however, are necessary but not sufficient to create a *habit* of co-operation. The fact is that even in the presence of consensus and common language a habit of non-cooperation is the rule. It seems to take a completely novel situation—a war, a McCarthy, a military government, a new mass medium, a severe depression—to give co-operation and hence applied science a chance. The reason, I believe, is that in such a novel situation, vested interests are less established. For in the last analysis, a habit of co-operation between scientist and executive can only prevail in a favorable and sensible power structure.

Such a power structure is illustrated by the context in which a Royal Commission in Britain operates.[3] Like Parliament and Cabinet its legitimization derives from the Crown. There are many trappings and ceremonies of prestige surrounding a Commission and it can command vast publicity. It is easy to understand why cabinets of either party are less than apt to ignore the recommendations made.

The British Royal Commission may also teach us a more important lesson: Its scientists are completely divorced from the responsibility for and risk in making the actual policy decision. Specialized scientists are called upon but usually remain in minority on the Commission or appear only as witnesses. The majority are lay members, drawn from the establishment itself, and appointed by the government of the day after consultation with opposition leaders. Furthermore, the actual decisions of implementation are taken outside the Commission by the Cabinet or by Parliament. This is where the occasional American practice of having professors in the White House and much of the current debate of

[3] See a forthcoming book by Dr. John Hanser.

184

the role of the social scientist in the U. S. government muddles important distinctions. In my opinion, a great effort must be made to distinguish the roles of the researcher and consultant on one hand and the role of decision maker on the other. It is essential to realize that use of social science in the shaping of policy decision—an idea which we advocate—is not at all the same thing as use of the social scientist as a policy and decision maker—an idea that I must admit leaves me very uncomfortable.

A scientist can aid a decision maker by providing the stuff out of which decisions are made—knowledge. He is competent by his training to provide this. But he is not particularly competent to make the decision itself; nothing in a researcher's or consultant's training has qualified him in any special way for such a task. Of course, one makes many decisions in the course of scientific work, decisions about methods, data inferences, conclusions and so forth. The interesting fact about these decisions is that they involve only modest risks and that these risks are borne by the scientist alone. If a wrong decision is made and a scientific mistake is published, the worst that can happen is that someone points out the error in a subsequent publication and the erring scientist stands corrected. This may be embarrassing and hurt one's professional reputation a little, but usually the scientist still has his job and his community

185

standing. It may sometimes even be an asset to him to have received the attention brought about by his mistake. In short, mistaken decisions have little consequence in the world of science; in that sense it is a gentle world.

By contrast, men in business, finance, government and the military pay dearly in money, career, social disorder, and human lives for their mistakes. Men devoted to careers in such fields, therefore, get a harsher training in decision making than do scientists. For this reason I advise that researchers and consultants leave the policy decisions to those better trained to bear the risks of such decisions. This admittedly unpopular advice is entirely compatible with sound sociological principles, and the one that a consultant is likely to arrive at, if he were asked about this problem.

Applied Research vs. Applied Theory

The scholarly consultation is a powerful procedure in the arsenal of social science. It may eventually replace many *ad hoc* research projects, which social scientists at present find necessary to use to answer problems presented by their clients. The advantages of the consultation over the project in cost, and in time required to deliver recommendations, are obvious. Research takes time and uses costly equipment. Consultations are cheaper and faster than research projects. Also, they are likely to be broader in scope. Applied research is always specialized research; the typical project gives information in terms of a few carefully measured and studied variables. In making policy, however, the executives are responsible for the effects of every decision on their total operations, not just the aspects studied. To the man, or board of men, who makes the ultimate decision, the researcher with the results of his project is usually just another voice to be listened to before the decision is reached or announced. This voice is one in the chorus of lawyers, public relations men, budget experts—not to speak of department heads with vested interests in the outcome of the decision. The social researcher is at a disadvantage in this company; he knows his few variables better than anyone, but these variables are only part of the picture. A sociological consultant, on the other hand, drawing on the rich tradition of his science, and knowledgeable of the total context in which a decision is being made, is in a different position. He is not only one voice among many demanding attention; he is, in effect, available as a confidant of the decision maker, helping to bring order and perspective to the other voices and helping him to weigh the different alternatives and their likely consequences. Probably, sociological consultations can influence the shape of policy easier than applied social research. I believe that consultations have an advantage over projects of applied research not only in terms of time and cost, but also in terms of their effect on policy.

The disadvantage of a consultation is its dependence on what is found in the tradition of a science. No consultation can be made on topics for which there is not already some available problem-relevant knowledge. A research project must be designed for such topics (*cf. supra,* p. 166). In principle, proponents of projects and proponents of consultations should be able to agree on a division of labor; however, since this division also involves a division of the client's dollars, disagreements are likely in practice.

The line becomes harder to draw on account of two complications. One is a common organizational pressure within research organizations devoted to applied research projects; when a project ends, the organization must find another one to be able to keep its staff. This tempts the organization to do new research on problems presented by clients, when science already knows the answer. These problems could have been solved by a simple consultation telling results of past research. However, that would mean idle staff members and research facilities, an unwanted prospect. Hence, research is recommended when a consultation would have been more appropriate. The second difficulty in getting a proper line drawn between the necessity for

188

consultation and the necessity for research stems from the consultants. They feel that they lose respect and future assignments if they admit that they do not know the answer to a problem. While the proper thing is to engage a researcher at any point of ignorance, the consultant is tempted to proceed by guesswork, thus making a mockery of his professed scientific approach.

In the last analysis, however, a promotion of applied social theory need not rest on its possible advantages over applied social research. The phrase "nothing is as practical as a good theory" is a twist of an older truth: Nothing improves theory more than its confrontation with practice. It is my belief that the development of applied social theory will do much good to basic theoretical sociology. This is obvious enough as we deal with those parts of theoretical sociology that are put to practical use; they become refined in the process.

Of course, there will always be the need for social theorists who work on basic problems which are unrelated to presently felt social problems. Even these pure sociological theoreticians can, however, profit from an environment in which social theory is applied to practical problems. Practical application of social theory sets good standards for theorizing: It forces theorists to be at least reasonably precise; to stay in close contact with reality; and to have more than a technical vocabulary to offer when talking about social events.

189

Applied social theory thus holds out prospects for improvements in the quality of theoretical sociology. One can only hope that these improvements will be of the same magnitude as those that applied social research in recent decades have brought to basic research techniques and methods.

Date Due

4/7/63			
APR 5 1982			

Library Bureau Cat. No. 1137